complete **cat care**

complete **cat care**

the essential guide to looking after your pet

author **Alan Edwards** veterinary consultant **Trevor Turner, B. VET. MED, F.R.S.H., M.R.C.V.S.**

southwater

This edition is published by Southwater

Distributed in the UK by
The Manning Partnership
251–253 London Road East
Batheaston
Bath BA1 7RL
tel. 01225 852 727
fax 01225 852 852

Distributed in Canada by
General Publishing
895 Don Mills Road
400–402 Park Centre
Toronto, Ontario M3C 1W3
tel. 416 445 3333
fax 416 445 5991

Published in the USA by
Anness Publishing Inc.
27 West 20th Street
Suite 504
New York, NY 10011
fax 212 807 6813

Distributed in Australia by
Sandstone Publishing
Unit 1, 360 Norton Street
Leichhardt
New South Wales 2040
tel. 02 9560 7888
fax 02 9560 7488

Southwater is an imprint of Anness Publishing Limited
Hermes House, 88–89 Blackfriars Road, London SE1 8HA
tel. 020 7401 2077; fax 020 7633 9499

© Anness Publishing Limited 2001

1 3 5 7 9 10 8 6 4 2

Publisher Joanna Lorenz
Managing Editor Judith Simons
Project Editor Mariano Kälfors
Designer Michael Morey
Jacket Design DW Design
Production Controller Yolande Denny
Editorial Reader Joy Wotton

Previously published as part of a larger compendium, *The Ultimate Encyclopedia of Cats, Cat Breeds and Cat Care.*

PICTURE CREDITS
All photography by John Daniels unless otherwise stated.
t=top; b=bottom; l=left; r=right; c=centre
AKG: 12 b. **Animals Unlimited**: 18 t; 24 t; 31 t; 36 t; 44 t, bl; 45 br; 46 t; 51 b; 52 b; 54 t, b; 60 t; 62 b; 64 c; 69 tr; 68 c, b; 73 c; 75t; 78 t, c; 84 t; 85 br; 89 c; 103 br; 124. **Janet Boswell**: 47 br; 50 br; 55 b; 60 b. **Bridgeman Art Library**: 13 b. **Chanan Photography, C.A.**: 53 c; 55 t; 56 b; 101 b. **Gilly Cameron Cooper**: 19 c; 23 t; 34 br; 45 bl; 62 t; 83 c; 85 tr; 99 tl; 112 br. **e.t. Archive**: 12 c. 13 t. **FLPA**: 8; 10 b; 11 t; 14 t; 15 c, b; 21 c; 23 b; 47 bc; 48 bl, br; 50 t; 51 t; 57 b; 58; 60 br; 64 t; 65 b; 84 bl; 86 t; 87 bl; 88 br; 90; 96 c; 109 t; 112 tl, tr, bl; 116 b; 118 t; 126 t. **Marc Henrie**: 16; 19 t; 92 c. **Mac on Mac Design**: 30 b; 49 t; 50 bl. **Papilio Photographic**: 9 tl, c, br. **Planet Earth**: 9 bl; 11 b. **Warren Photographic**: 6; 18 b; 22t; 25; 26 t; 28; 29 t, c; 31 b; 40 t, br; 41 b; 42; 44 cr; 45 t; 47 t, bl; 48 t; 49 b; 60 c; 63 tl, r; 65 t; 67 bl, br; 68 t; 69 br; 70; 72 t, bl, br; 74 b; 78 bl, br; 79 tr, c, b; 83 bl; 85 tl; 87 tr; 88 t, bl; 89 tr, b; 92 t; 94 t, bl, br; 95 t, b; 96 bl; 98 t, b; 101 t; 102 t, bl, br; 103 tr, bl; 104; 109 b; 114; 115; 118 b; 120 bl; 121 bl, br; 122; 123; 125.

Contents

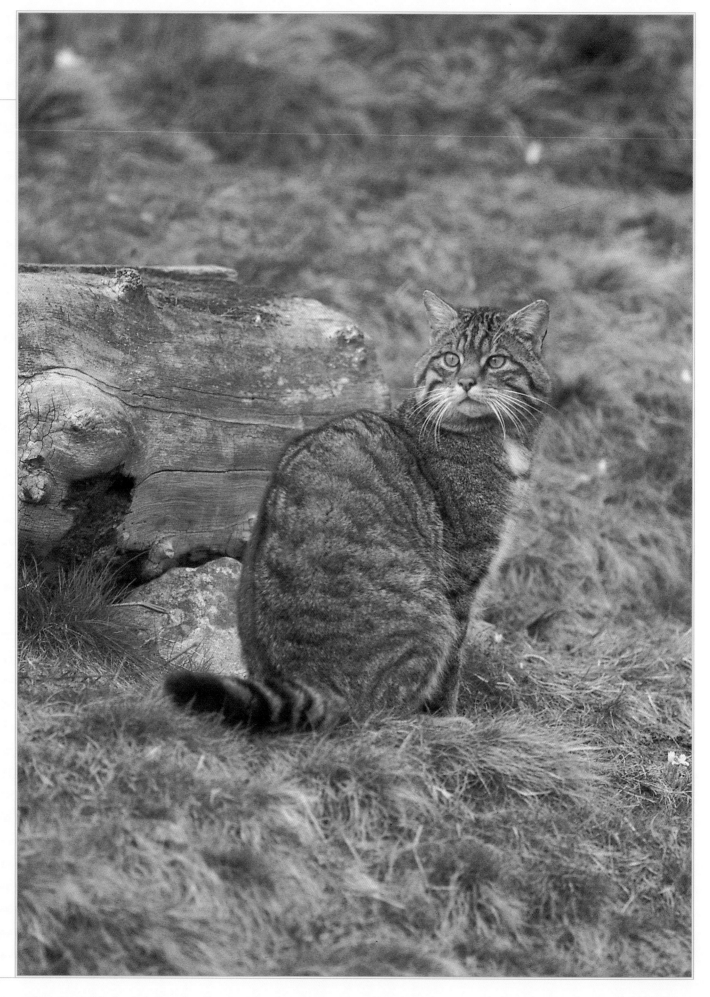

Introducing the Domestic Cat

Despite its obvious liking for comfort and human company, the domestic cat has many of the same characteristics as its wild relations. It shares the lithe muscularity of a body built for stalking and hunting and a fine-furred pelt with the big roaring cats of jungle and savanna. In fact, there are smaller wild species that have at times left their feral state to cohabit with humans. At this level, the boundaries between wildness and domesticity remain fluid. For although the domestic feline appears to have a smaller brain than its wild counterpart, if forced by circumstance, it can quite easily revert to the free-roaming, independent life of a wild predator.

◆ FACING PAGE
The European wild cat looks as though it might be related to the domestic tabby cat, but its wariness and untamed character are quite different.

◆ LEFT
The modern Bengal breed is a cross between a domestic cat and the wild Asian leopard cat (*Felis bengalensis*).

JOURNEY FROM THE WILD

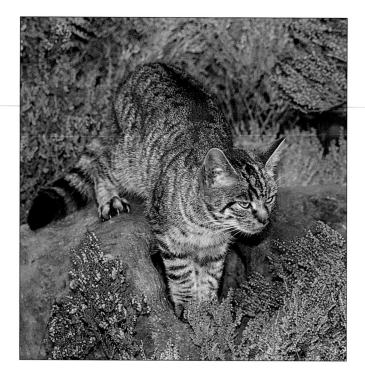

♦ LEFT AND BELOW
The European wild cat (*left*) was thought to be the ancestor of today's domestic cat because of its tabby markings, but this is now considered unlikely because of its instinctive wariness of people. The more likely contender is the African wild cat (*below*).

Members of the cat family Felidae range from the great, roaring cats such as the lion and tiger to the small domestic cat. They are separated into different genuses (family sub-divisions), not because of their size, but because of differences in their anatomy. These enable members of the genus *Panthera* to roar, while the small cats in genus *Felis* cannot do so. There is a third genus for the cheetahs because they have non-retractable claws. Early in the 1900s there were more than 230 different species of cat in the family as a whole, but now there are fewer than 30. Many became extinct because cats have always been hunted and killed by humans for their fine pelts.

ORIGINS OF DOMESTIC CATS

There is a close relationship between the wild and the domestic cat, but it is uncertain which wild sub-species of the *Felis* (small cats) genus actually made the leap into domesticity. Wild cats are widely distributed and vary considerably in appearance and habits. Northern cats, for example, developed dense, almost woolly coats, while in warmer, southern climes, a fine, body-hugging fur was the norm. Experts ended up with three major contenders for the ancestor of the domestic cat: the European wild cat and its Asian and African equivalents.

For many years, the Europeans believed that it was their wild cat (*Felis sylvestris sylvestris*), which is still found in localized parts of the Scottish Highlands and northern continental Europe. Their assumption was based on the cat's colouring and tabby markings that are common in non-pedigreed cats of today. However, even if the young offspring are reared by humans, they remain very wary, and do not abandon their wild behaviour patterns. This inherent anti-social streak makes them unlikely to have been inclined towards domestication.

On the other hand, the African wild cat (*F. sylvestris libyca*), which still survives in Africa, western Asia and southern Europe, not only has the same number of chromosomes as the domestic cat but is relatively

CAT ANCESTRY

The wild ancestors of today's domestic cat were among the first carnivores that evolved during the late Eocene and early Oligocene periods of pre-history over 35 million years ago. But it was another family of carnivores, the dogs, Canidae, that became the first animal companions of human beings. Stone Age man took advantage of the dog's superior sensory

powers to help him hunt, and this provided a sound basis for an ongoing relationship. It was not until people graduated into a more settled agricultural way of life that cats became part of the domestic scene.

Small feline skeletons have been found in Stone Age archaeological sites, usually with the remains of other small wild animals such as badgers, which suggests that the cats were killed for their meat or pelts. The first evidence of cats actually living in some tentative relationship with humans was found in a New Stone Age site in Jericho in the Middle East, dating from about 9,000 years ago. However, it is unlikely that domestic cats, living in a relationship with humans similar to that of today, emerged until around 3,500 years ago in ancient Egypt.

```
                    CLASS MAMMALIA
          ┌──────────────┴──────────────┐
   ORDER HERBIVORA                 ORDER CARNIVORA
    (Herbivores)                     (Carnivores)
                              ┌───────────┴───────────┐
                                  Family Felidae
                                      (Cats)
          ┌───────────────────────┼───────────────────────┐
       Panthera                  Felis                 Acinonyx
    (roaring cats)            (small cats)            (cat with
  including lion, leopard,                          non-retractable
     tiger, snow leopard,                               claws)
     jaguar, clouded leopard
                                                         │
                                                       cheetah

    ┌──────────────────────────────────────────────────────┐
  Felis manul                      Felis sylvestris libyca (African wild cat³)
   Manul²                          Felis sylvestris sylvestris (European wild cat¹)
                          and many other small cat species
```

1 May have bred with the early domesticated cats that reached Europe
2 A possible ancestor of longhaired cats
3 The most likely ancestor of most domestic cats

+ ABOVE LEFT
The leopard is in a different genus from the small cat not because it is bigger, but because the anatomy of its larynx enables it to roar.

+ RIGHT
Every member, big and small, of the cat family is built to be an efficient killer. The tiger, the largest of the *Panthera* species, is one of the most powerful predators of all.

The lion is another roaring cat of the genus *Panthera*. However, it is quite clearly in the same family as the domestic cat, with its flexible, muscular body, a typically short, rounded head, and large eyes.

The cheetah is in a separate genus because it has non-retractable claws. However, it is closely related to the puma (also known as the mountain lion or cougar), which can retract its claws.

sociable. Both this sub-species and the Asian desert cat (*F. sylvestris ornata*) often live on the outskirts of human settlements and are fairly easily tamed. Significantly, remains of the African wild cat have been found in caves lived in by ancient man, and it is generally accepted as the ancestor of most of today's domestic cats. *F. sylvestris libyca* (abbreviated to *F. libyca*) is, in fact, very similar to the Abyssinian breed of today – lithe, long-faced with large ears, and with a ticked, or agouti (dark-tipped) tan coat.

THE PATH TO DOMESTICATION

Our ancestors may simply have hunted and killed these cats, both as a food source and for their pelts. However, as humans were developing an agrarian society based on crops that would have attracted rodents, it

is also possible that the kittens were tamed and used to control pests. This would also have been in the cat's interests – keeping the scavenger population under control provided a regular concentration of well-fed prey.

In 1865, Francis Galton, a British scientist who specialized in the study of heredity and intelligence, defined the essential qualities of the early domestic animal. It would need to be useful, easy to tend, able to breed freely, and above all (in the case of

the dog and cat, for example), be comfort loving and have a liking for humans. There is also a hypothesis that the process of domestication from wild, savage feline may have been accelerated by genetic mutation. Genes, the building blocks for a living creature, include patterns for behaviour as well as the size and general conformation of the adult. A fault in the genes that control behaviour patterns could, at some time, have created a cat that was

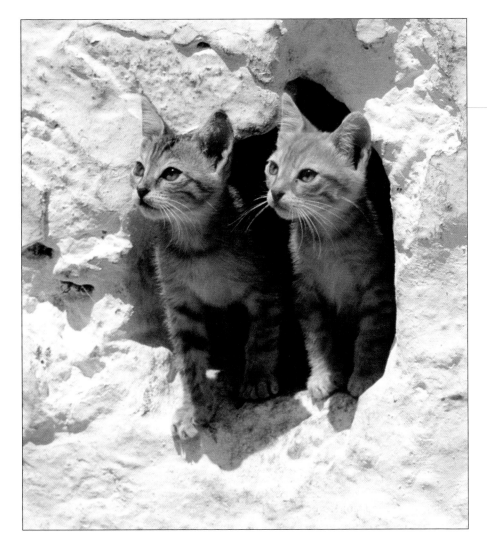

coat qualities that resemble those of the modern domesticated cat. It also seems that in such cross-matings, the genetic trait for domestication in one sub-species can strongly affect a more savage temperament in the other. The most recent example of this is the domestic cross with *F. bengalensis bengalensis* (Asian leopard cat) to produce the pedigree variety known as the Bengal. Successive generations enhanced the domesticated qualities of this new breed. (The registration organizations for pedigreed cats in some countries, notably the Cat Fanciers' Association in the United States, do not recognize this breed or any other developed from cross-matings of domestic cats with wild cats, although the Governing Council of the Cat Fancy in the United Kingdom does.)

temperamentally unwilling to leave a juvenile (kittenish) dependency state. This, coupled with a ready supply of food from the human farmers, created an environment in which the mutual advantages of domestication were explored. The kitten-cat gained warmth, comfort and a secure environment in which to breed, and its offspring were valued as an ongoing supply of rodent exterminators. This made the spread of the genetic fault creating the socially valuable domesticated cat inevitable.

The domestication process may well have been accelerated as the African wild cat spread from warm southern and eastern regions and cross-mated with its northern European relation. It has been found recently that cross-matings of these sub-species produce animals with

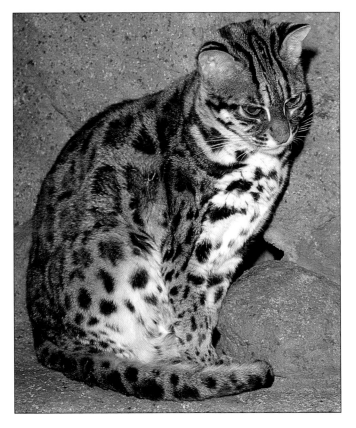

◆ LEFT
The Asian leopard cat (*Felis bengalensis bengalensis*) is a wild species that has been crossed with a domestic cat to produce a new pedigree, the Bengal.

◆ LEFT
Ancient Egyptian murals depict cats well settled into domestic life. This one has tabby stripes on its back – the most common fur pattern that is also seen on the African wild cat.

◆ BELOW
A mummified cat discovered in an Egyptian tomb dating from between 1000 and 332 BC. More than 300,000 cat mummies were discovered at one archaeological site in 1890.

MEDITERRANEAN REFINEMENT

Compared with the dog, the domestication of the cat is relatively recent. It probably occurred only 5–8,000 years ago, compared with the dog's 50,000-year relationship with humans. During excavations of the 8,000-year-old human settlement of Khirokitia in Cyprus in 1983, a single feline jawbone was found. Cyprus has never had endemic wild cats, so it is possible that this cat was a domestic animal. The proximity of Cyprus to Africa suggests that it could have been related to the African wild cat *F. sylvestris libyca*.

However, overwhelming evidence points to ancient Egypt as the first area in which the cat was elevated to a role beyond that of rodent exterminator. The cat established a niche for itself in ancient Egypt as

◆ BELOW
This polished bronze statue of Bastet, the cat goddess of ancient Egypt, dates from the 6th century BC and stands 34cm (13½in) high.

early as 3500 BC. Wall paintings in tombs built at the time of the New Kingdom (1560–1080 BC) depict the cat as being part of daily Egyptian life. On the death of a household cat, Egyptian families went into deep mourning, shaving off their eyebrows as a sign of their grief.

The cat was also revered as a symbol of fertility. Bastet (also known as Bast and Pasht), daughter of the sun god Re, or Osiris, and goddess of

◆ RIGHT

A cat is featured in a 13th-century bestiary (a book of beasts). Although widely feared and reviled at this time, cats were still useful mousers, and in England, were protected by the Church to some extent.

fertility, was originally depicted as a lion, but later assumed the shape of a small cat. It is from her name that the word puss is thought to derive.

In 1890, archaeologists discovered more than 300,000 cat mummies buried in an underground sanctuary dedicated to Bastet at Ben Hassan. Beside the cat mummies were mummified mice – food for the cats' journey into the afterlife. Cats were also domesticated in the Far East in ancient times, probably around 2000 BC. They may have arisen from the Asian desert cat (*F. sylvestris ornata*) and be the forebears of the longhaired domestic cat.

TRADE WITH ROME

The domesticated cat in the West spread with the expansion of the Roman Empire. Romans smuggled

cats out of Egypt and took them to their northern conquests, where they were used to control rodents. Cats also enjoyed some degree of veneration by the Romans. The 1st-century BC Greek historian Diodorus describes an incident in which a Roman charioteer in Alexandria, who ran over and killed a cat, was stoned to death by an angry mob.

Monks travelling to the Far East took cats with them, where they would have bred with the Asian domestic cats. The earliest domestic cat bone discovered in Britain dates back to between AD 10 and AD 43, before the Roman conquest. In Chelmsford, England, Roman roof tiles impressed with cats' paw prints have been found.

MEDIEVAL IMAGE CRISIS

The Romans saw the cat as a symbol of liberty. It was with the fall of the Roman Empire that the cat lost popularity. Earlier beliefs were adapted to fit in with the cat's gradual loss of image. The northern goddess of love, Freya, for example, had always

◆ BELOW

By the time this cat was depicted in a 14th-century bestiary, the cat population was declining due to persecution. This helped the rodent population spread, and with it the virus that carried the Black Death through Europe.

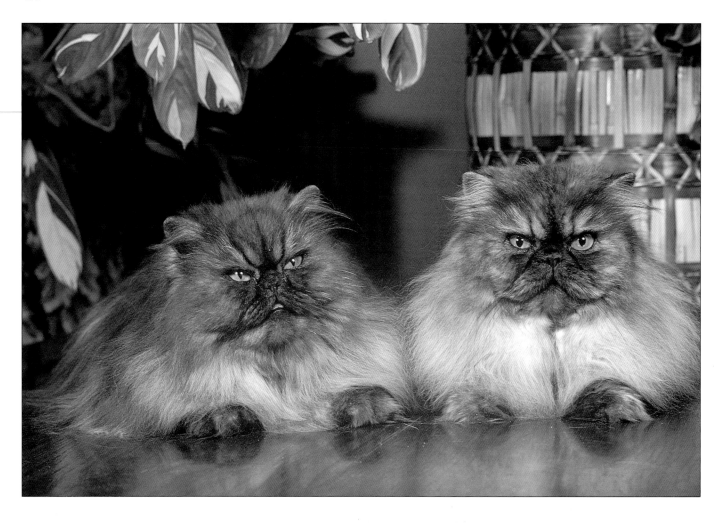

been depicted surrounded by cats, but later became a frightening witch whose cats were the denizens of hell. For around 700 years after the first millennium, throughout Europe the cat was often associated with witches and evil. In the town of Metz in France, hundreds of cats were burned alive on the second Wednesday in Lent, as a ritual sacrifice of witches.

In parts of the post-Roman world, the cat disappeared completely from the archaeological records. Luckily, in Britain it was still highly valued as a mouser, and until the 10th century – the beginning of the Middle Ages – it enjoyed some protection from the Church. However, in continental Europe, its fur was used to line and decorate garments, including the trimmings on the gowns of lawyers. In times of famine, cat flesh was added to the soups and stews of hungry farming folk.

◆ ABOVE
Persian cats were among the first exotic breeds to be developed in the West, their popularity boosted by the enthusiasm of European royals such as Queen Victoria of England.

◆ BELOW
The Maine Coon Cat was a valuable mouser in the north-eastern United States, and was a major winner at America's first cat show in Madison Square Garden, New York in 1895.

A NEW ERA

From the 1600s, the cat did once again find some favour as a domestic pet. The French Cardinal Richelieu was known to like cats, which he had with him while he worked. A French harpist left a large part of her fortune to her cats, together with instructions that they be properly cared for. By the 1700s, cats were sometimes featured in portraits of the Romantic era as favoured companions, and the poet Thomas Gray wrote his *Ode on the Death of A Favourite Cat Drowned in a Tub of Goldfishes*. There was even a cat fair held in the city of Winchester, England in 1598.

However, it was not until the 1800s that serious interest was taken. Country fairs in the United States included exhibitions of Maine Coon Cats from the 1860s. A cat show proper, with Maine Coons featuring strongly, was held in Madison Square

✦ RIGHT
Domestic cats now outnumber dogs as favourite
pets. In the United States the cat population is
around 56 million compared with 54 million
dogs, in Britain, 7.5 million against 6.7 million.

Garden in New York in 1895. The first
British cat show – with benched cats
in individual pens – was held at
London's Crystal Palace in 1871. It
was organized by the writer and
notable cat artist Harrison Weir. The
early shows were inspired by a
growing interest in the glamorous
pedigreed breeds. It became necessary
for some sort of registration body to
record the parentage of the cats, and
to set some sort of standard that
would list the desirable and
undesirable traits for each breed. This
was the role of the National Cat Club,
founded in the United Kingdom in
1887, which marked the beginning of
the cat fancy as it is known today.
Harrison Weir was its first president.

Local clubs and clubs for specific
breeds were soon formed. Today,
there are active cat fancies in most
countries, recent additions being
Russia and Malaysia. At the early

✦ ABOVE
The Turkish Angora of today is very different
from its late-19th-century ancestor that,
together with a Persian cat, founded many of
the modern longhaired cat breeds.

shows, the main varieties seen were
Persian longhairs, domestic shorthairs,
Siamese, Foreign Blue (now known as
Russian Blue), Manx and Abyssinian.
During the 1900s, as travel became
easier, wealthy enthusiasts imported
cats from other countries and different
breeds quickly spread across the
world. Breeding suffered a setback
during the world wars, and some
breeds, such as the Abyssinian and
Russian Blue, nearly became extinct.
From the late 1950s, the cat fancy and
knowledge of genetics grew, and many
new breeds and colour varieties within
breeds were developed.

✦ RIGHT
Although cats are
described as domestic
pets, as a species they
can readily return to
the wild and survive
(although a
pampered, highly
bred individual
might have
difficulty). This
creates a feral (wild)
population like these
residents of a
Greek island.

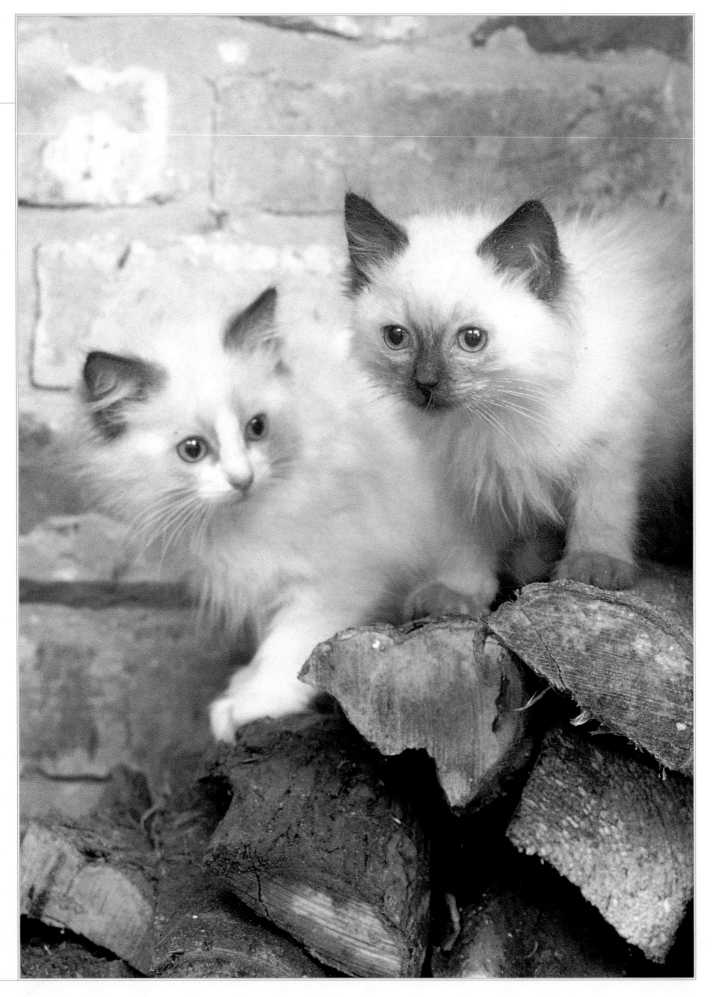

Choosing the Right Cat

Many households are entirely suitable for a cat, or even a companionable pair of cats, but it is important to consider the effects a cat will have on the household. Although they are known for their independence of character, cats do need care and attention. A normal, healthy cat may live for fourteen years or more, and you need to consider whether you can stand such a long-term responsibility and commitment. Cats may all be roughly the same size and shape, but they vary a great deal in temperament, interests and needs. Before you buy a cat, it is wise to look at your lifestyle and home, and consider the type of cat that will happily fit in with it.

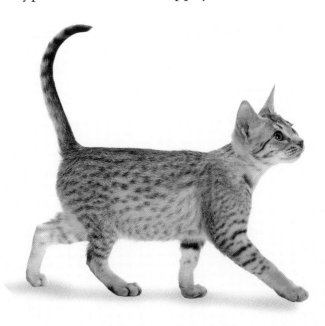

◆ FACING PAGE
Ragdoll kittens like these will grow into calm, good-natured adults that enjoy comfort and should adapt happily to an indoor lifestyle.

◆ LEFT
A lively Ocicat may not be of the ideal temperament to be confined to an indoor life.

17

WHY CHOOSE A CAT?

The cat's adaptability and independence make it a very practical pet for the modern working household. Cats do not have to be taken for walks; they self-clean and self-exercise. Some can happily adjust to a life spent totally indoors in a high-rise apartment. Depending on their character (and breed type if they are purebred), they can also learn to live with other domestic pets. For many people, though, it is the beauty of the cat that is so alluring. A cat on watch at a window, on the prowl or playing in the garden, or simply as a soothing, sleeping presence, is a graceful and rewarding, easy-care asset to the home and family.

THE RIGHT CAT

The choice of cat depends very much on personal preference for a particular type of cat, for long or short fur, or a particular coat colour and pattern. A

✦ ABOVE
Cat and bird, as well as dog and cat, are legendary enemies, but it need not be so. Cats can be persuaded to live harmoniously with other domestic pets.

✦ LEFT
A pair of farm kittens on an old tractor wheel look irresistible. They may grow up to be much-loved pets, but will probably also earn their keep as valuable mousers.

♦ RIGHT
A purebred cat with a pedigree will cost considerably more to acquire than a non-pedigreed animal, and caring for it may be a lot more time-consuming.

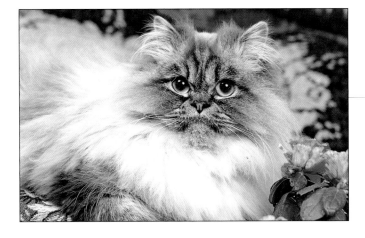

major determining factor is how much you want to spend. At the top end of the price scale are cats whose parents and grandparents can be traced through long pedigrees back to the late 1800s. At the other end of the scale are unplanned litters of non-pedigreed cats which may be picked up for free. In between are cross-breeds – a random or deliberate result of a mating between different breeds, or the unplanned mating of one pedigreed partner with a non-pedigree. At a fraction of the cost of a true pedigree, you could have a cat with the aristocratic qualities of its purebred mother and the resilient health of its father, or vice versa.

Size is not an issue. Unlike dogs, domestic cats do not vary greatly in size – there is no feline equivalent of the Great Dane or the tiny Chihuahua. Living-space restrictions do not generally present a problem as cats are very adaptable. Allowances need to be made for some active breeds, but most cats can settle into a small apartment as happily as into a large house.

THE PEDIGREE OPTION

Buying a purebred dog from a reputable breeder has long been accepted. However, it is only comparatively recently that interest in pedigreed cats has become established. Until about 30 years ago, there was a scarcity of breeders and, with the exception of Blue Persian and Siamese breeds, pedigreed cats were not readily

♦ ABOVE
Feral cats can be picked up for free on many a Mediterranean island, but they need particularly careful medical attention.

♦ BELOW
The non-pedigree from a known background is cheap and likely to be balanced of character and sturdy of health.

available. This situation has been radically redressed by the cat fancy (the world of pedigreed cats) being much more active in its publicity. The showing and breeding of cats with a known ancestry has become a popular hobby, making a much greater range of breeds available.

A key advantage of buying a pedigreed kitten from a reputable breeder is that there are safeguards woven into the transaction.

OFF THE STREETS

Cats that have been abandoned by their owners, or that have been born on the streets, carve a life for themselves as strays. They revert to a feral (wild) state, form colonies with other cats, and breed prolifically. It is perfectly possible to adopt a stray or feral cat you have found on the streets. One might even adopt you. However, they have been exposed to a host of infections and diseases, so thorough medical examination and inoculation is particularly important. You will also need to spend more time with a stray to help it bond with you and adjust to a settled way of life.

LONGHAIR OR SHORTHAIR?

Having a longhaired cat requires you to set aside some time every day to groom it, to keep the coat free from tangles and matting. At the other extreme, the almost hairless Sphynx cat needs extra care as it is very susceptible to temperature change and skin problems.

If you are living in a hot, humid climate, a longhaired cat (even if it sheds its cold-weather coat) is not a wise choice unless it is to live in an air-conditioned home. The coat of a Sphynx does not adapt at all to climatic changes, and the cat would need to be kept in a centrally heated environment in cold winters.

If you are allergic to cats, it will probably make no difference whether you have a longhair or a shorthair. Most human allergies to cats are due to the proteins in the scurf (dander) or in the dried saliva covering the hair.

◆ ABOVE
The Maine Coon Cat is a breed with a semi-longhaired coat, which will not need as much extra care as the long fur of a Persian cat.

◆ BELOW
The fur of the Devon Rex cat is fine and wavy and can be so delicate in places that it is broken just by the cat's own grooming. Grooming should be with a very soft bristled brush.

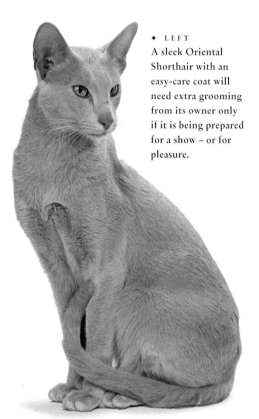

◆ LEFT
A sleek Oriental Shorthair with an easy-care coat will need extra grooming from its owner only if it is being prepared for a show – or for pleasure.

◆ RIGHT
This Persian cat has a splendid long coat that requires a lot of attention. If it lived in a hot climate, however, it would not develop such a full "show" coat.

FUR TYPES

Longhair: soft guardhairs up to 12.5cm (5in) long

Semi-longhair: soft guardhairs varying between 5cm (2in) and 10cm (4in) long

Shorthair: maximum about 5cm (2in) long

Hairless: suede-like coat with no guardhairs

Curly hair: short, soft, often delicate fur with rippled effect

Wirehair: short, bristly coat

BODY TYPES

Cobby: short-legged, stocky body; round, flattish face with small ears, such as the Persian

Muscular: sturdy, medium to compact build; medium length legs and tail; round face, medium ears, such as the American Shorthair

Oriental: long, lithe body; long, slender legs and tail; wedge-shaped face; large, pointed ears, such as the Siamese

GENDER AND AGE

If cats are neutered (altered), there is little difference in behavioural terms between a male and a female. However, a neutered male may be a little more indolent than a female. If you already have a cat in your home, it may be worth going for the opposite sex in your new cat. The established resident is more likely to defend its territory aggressively against a cat of the same sex.

Once sexual urges have been quelled by the neutering process, cats are likely to exhibit their true breed characteristics more strongly. The Siamese cat's attachment to its owner is accentuated, for example, and the Persian becomes even more placid and comfort-loving.

Male cats are generally larger than females. On average, a full-grown, neutered male cat tends to be a little heavier than an entire male, with an average weight of between 5 and 7.5kg (10–15lb). Females are usually about 1kg (2.2lb) lighter. The largest pedigreed variety is the Maine Coon Cat from the north-eastern United States. Male Maine Coons have been

◆ RIGHT
A kitten will adapt to your lifestyle more readily than an older cat, simply because it has not yet fully developed its mature character.

known to reach about 10–12.5kg (20–25lb) in weight. The smallest, or most dainty breed is the Singapura (the "drain cat" of Singapore) at about 2.7kg (6lb), but breeders take care to make certain that their cats fall within the minimum weight range to ensure successful breeding.

◆ ABOVE
Male cats are usually bigger than their female equivalents, although if they have been neutered (altered), they may be a little more indolent.

CHOOSING AN ADULT CAT

It can be easier to give a new home to an older cat than to a kitten. This is especially so if the cat is obtained from a major welfare source which has carried out rigorous health checks. (With a kitten from a private home, the onus of the initial health checks is usually left to you.) An older animal will be more settled in its ways and certainly have an established temperament. A poor temperament due to the cat coming from an environment where it was unhappy, can improve with changed circumstances, but you do not have the fresh start you would have with a kitten. Male cats that have only recently been neutered (altered) may carry some battle scars from their fighting days, but this is a purely aesthetic consideration.

◆ RIGHT
Although the Singapura may have evolved into one of the smallest breeds because of its tough background on the streets of Singapore, it is a sturdy animal.

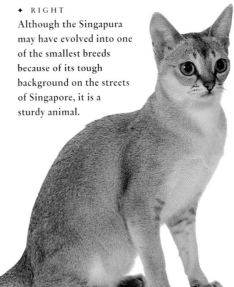

◆ ABOVE
Deciding to take in an adult cat that you have found in a cat sanctuary or home may save the animal from being humanely put to sleep, and it will soon learn to be content in its new, welcoming environment.

WHERE TO FIND A HEALTHY KITTEN

It is essential to choose a healthy kitten. One picked up from the street should be approached with caution.

Despite the pro-neutering campaigns of welfare agencies, unneutered (unaltered) cats do roam freely. This, together with the rapid maturation of the cat, makes it possible for a four-month-old to become pregnant, resulting in the next generation. Such kittens may not be physically strong, they may have been separated from their mother too soon, and are unlikely to have had any veterinary attention or inoculations. Diseases such as feline influenza and feline enteritis can strike a very young kitten and kill rapidly. In addition, feline immunodeficient diseases (feline Aids) may be present.

ACCEPTABLE FREE GIFTS

Some owners allow their cats to have one litter before neutering, and then offer the kittens "free to a good home". They may ask searching questions about your ability to look after the kittens well. Take this in good grace, for these are people who want the best for their kittens.

◆ ABOVE
These two farm kittens probably come from a long line of good hunters. Their strength is largely dependent on the physical well-being of their mother and her ability to rear them successfully until weaned.

◆ LEFT
A kitten is hand-fed using a syringe and a special formula milk, as the mother has either died or is unable to take care of her litter.

◆ ABOVE RIGHT
The weight of the hand-reared kitten is checked daily. It needs to gain about 9g (⅓oz) a day, and to be kept constantly warm.

CAT HOMES

If you want to give a home to an unwanted cat or kitten, go to a welfare agency or humane society. There are several big, well-known national organizations as well as many smaller charities that cater for homeless or unwanted cats.

Cats are not usually released to a new owner until they have been given a veterinary check, but the organization may not have had the time or resources for full investigations. This is particularly the case with feline immunodeficiency disease or feline Aids, the test for which is quite expensive. However, coats are routinely checked for parasites and fungal conditions, and the usual vaccinations are often given.

The main welfare organizations usually do investigate thoroughly, including blood-tests to ensure feline

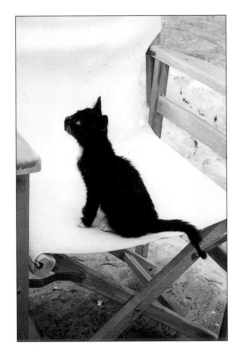

✦ ABOVE
A tiny stray kitten may not be very strong or healthy as it was probably abandoned by its mother too soon – and the mother herself is unlikely to have been in top condition.

Aids and leukaemia are not present. In addition, once an animal has been chosen, they visit the home of the prospective new owner to ensure that it is suitable. Such attention to detail means that they may charge for the kitten, which may make the potential owner think twice before buying. But whatever the cost, it is certainly less than the cost of bringing a stray in dubious condition to peak fitness.

Some pet shops offer kittens for sale only after the necessary veterinary checks and inoculations have been done. However, for the kitten, the stress of leaving its mother, being in the shop, and then being sold on to yet another new environment within a very short time can set them back developmentally. By law in the United Kingdom, kittens must not be sold under six weeks of age. If they appear tiny, it is wise not to purchase.

✦ RIGHT
The last kitten left in a pet shop pen may look appealing, but think carefully before you buy. Will it have picked up parasites from other animals in the shop? Did it have the right medical checks and inoculations before it was put up for sale?

WHERE TO FIND A PEDIGREED CAT

Some breeders advertise in local newspapers. This is a rather hit-and-miss source as there are no guarantees that they are reputable. Some unscrupulous breeders produce kittens of the most popular breeds purely for profit. They may show little concern for either the future welfare of the offspring, or for the breed as a whole.

A far better idea is to ask at your local veterinary surgery or clinic for information on those in the area who specialize in various breeds. Often, if one breeder has no kittens available at the time you want one, he or she will recommend another. Some breeders operate on a large scale and have big catteries, while others are "front parlour" breeders, who may be interested in breeding from just one pet queen. Either can be a good source; the best way to find out about them is by recommendation via a vet

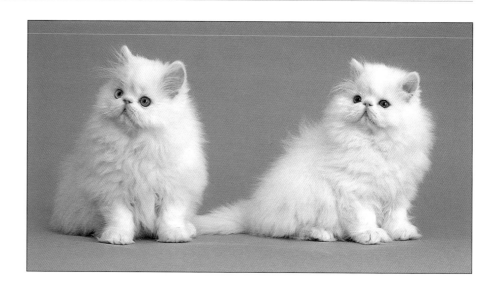

or a local breed club. It is also valuable to visit cat shows well before you actually buy. Here you will find enthusiastic owners and breeders who will explain the advantages and disadvantages of their favourite breeds and let you know of available stock. Find out about cat shows from one of the specialist cat magazines.

◆ ABOVE
The charms of a pedigreed kitten are displayed by these two White Persians. If you want information about where to buy cats like this, the best place to start is the breed club.

◆ BELOW
The Supreme Show is where you can see the best examples of all the pedigreed breeds in the United Kingdom. There are cat shows in most countries at breed club, local and national levels.

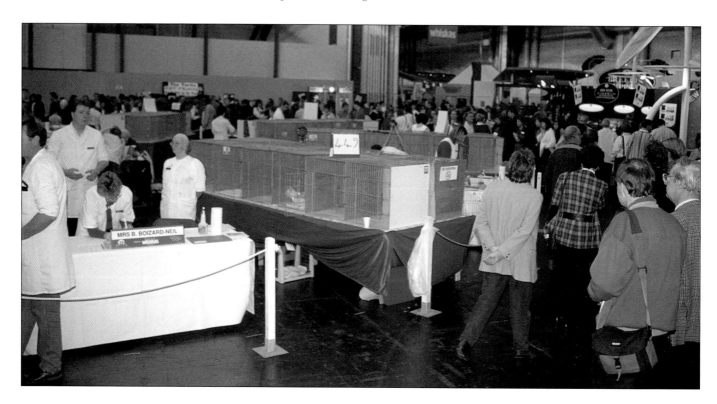

VISITING THE BREEDER

Some breeders house their animals in an outside cattery, others within their homes. A reputable breeder will not hesitate to allow a prospective owner to visit. The advantage of the house-reared litter is that the kittens are socialized earlier. They have greater contact with day-to-day noise, humans and perhaps other animals such as dogs. On the other hand, the disinfection and restricted contact routine of a first-rate cattery reduces the risk of disease and infection. Kittens from a good cattery will be handled and socialized, but this process cannot be as complete as if they were raised within the home. Beware of the unscrupulous cattery owner rearing kittens solely for financial gain. Conditions can often be substandard.

Usually, you need to make an appointment to see and select from a litter of kittens, but it is also possible to book a kitten in advance of delivery if you are drawn to a particular cat. By visiting the breeder, you can assess the general environment and conditions in which the kittens have been brought up in the first few vital weeks of their lives. If you ask the right questions and see the rest of the litter, the mother, and possibly the father, you will be able to build up a complete picture of the kitten's heritage – its breeding line; how long its relatives have lived; how big it is likely to grow; what it will look like as an adult. In addition, you can lay the foundations of an ongoing relationship with the breeder, who, if reputable, will be available for advice and help in the years to come.

A pedigreed kitten will not usually leave its breeder's home until it is twelve to fourteen weeks old. By this time it should be properly house-trained, inoculated and used to being handled. If it has been brought up in a family environment, it may already be happy with dogs and children. But if it has not been in an ideal environment, it may have difficulties bonding with a new owner. In this case (and with a non-pedigreed kitten only) it may adapt more easily if it is taken away at seven or eight weeks.

A kitten ready for handing over to a new owner should have been gently weaned and introduced to a suitable diet of fresh, canned and dry foods. It should have been registered with one or more of the many registering bodies worldwide and the registration documents and pedigree should be ready to take away. There may also be a health insurance policy that lasts about six weeks – enough time to let the new kitten settle into its new home.

The cost of a pedigreed kitten depends very much on the breed; seek guidelines from the individual breed clubs. It is possible to spend a great deal of money on rare, new varieties while the well-established, popular varieties are less expensive. Kittens of show quality are priced more highly than those of lesser quality.

♦ BELOW
Kittens being prepared to leave their breeders for a new home. If they have become used to a friendly family environment from birth, they should settle down quickly.

SELECTING A HEALTHY ANIMAL

A kitten from a responsible breeder will have had trips to the vet for inoculations against cat flu, feline infectious enteritis, and possibly chlamydia and feline leukaemia. It will have been wormed and its coat will be free from parasites (such as fleas) and fungal lesions (ringworm).

The queen passes on natural immunity to the diseases to which she is herself immune, through colostrum (first milk) during the kitten's first few days of life. This immunity is effective until the kitten is six to ten weeks of age, when it must be replaced by the artificially acquired immunity provided by inoculations. Before the age of eight or nine weeks, it is best not to interfere with the immunity acquired from the mother.

It is not advisable to take the kitten home before inoculations start if you have other cats. They might be carriers of feline diseases to which the mother of the kitten is not immune

✦ ABOVE
You may be tempted to buy both of these kittens. They have grown up together so are likely always to be friendly. They will enjoy playing together – and you will enjoy watching them. Make sure both are neutered, however!

✦ BELOW
At nine weeks old these non-pedigreed kittens could be taken from their birth home. However, some cat associations recommend they are left until 12 weeks, after the first vaccination course has finished.

and against which, therefore, the kitten has no protection. The certificate from the vet confirming first or complete vaccination carries with it the important implication that the cat is in good health – otherwise the inoculation would not have been administered.

WHAT TO LOOK FOR

The prospective owner can make his or her own immediate checks when selecting a kitten. If you are able to view the entire litter, look for the individuals with evenness of growth and solidity of muscle tone. Male kittens may already be showing a larger skeletal frame than the females. The kittens will be heavy for their size, and their spines should be well-fleshed and not feel ridged and bony.

If you see the litter shortly after feeding, the kittens will probably be sleepy, but if they are inclined to play, you can assess sociability. Frightened, unsociable kittens rush to hide and show fear and displeasure with trembling, bad language or claws – or maybe all three at once! The sociable but sleepy kitten purrs and almost certainly demands that its tummy is tickled. The playful kitten in good health has stamina and a spring in its step. It is alert and may already be displaying intelligence and leadership in play. Rather than you doing the choosing, a particular kitten may well choose you, inviting you to play, and ending up going to sleep on your lap.

The kitten's nose leather should be naturally slightly warm and a little damp. It should not be hot and dry, or have any discoloured discharge from the nostrils. Breathing should be deep and natural with no rasping or snorting. Eyes should be clean and bright with no discharge, tears, staining or redness. The mouth should show nice light-pink gums with no furring to the tongue or ulceration. Ears should be clean and free of wax.

COAT INDICATORS

Clean kitten fur has a lively feel with a warm, naturally wholesome scent, with no evidence of parasites, rough patches or lesions. The most common ectoparasite is the flea, which leaves gritty, granular droppings. Typical sites for these droppings are just above the base of the tail, between the shoulder blades, under the chin and in the armpits. Excessive infestation of fleas may cause a lack of liveliness, and also indicate that the animal may be worm-infested.

Signs of worm infestation are commonly a staring, harsh coat and a bloated abdomen. In severe cases, the kitten may show signs of anaemia and

◆ ABOVE
This Chocolate Silver Tabby Ocicat not only has fine tabby markings, but his clear, bright eyes suggest he is in peak health.

diarrhoea. Check under the tail for staining or signs of soreness, which indicate diarrhoea.

CHECKING AN ADULT CAT

The health check for the older cat is much the same. You need to check that male cats have been neutered (altered). If this has happened recently, they may show some battle scars, but this will only affect their appearance. The most likely place for wear and tear to show is in the mouth. Teeth may be missing or broken, and the gums may show signs of disease, but this can be treated by your vet, who may advise home dental care.

Whatever the age of the kitten or older cat you are thinking of buying, however sweet and charming it is, if you have any doubts about its health, and especially if you have other cats, do not take it home with you.

◆ BELOW
A confident stride, intelligent interest and a perky tail indicate that this 15-week-old Ocicat is a cat of sociable, playful character.

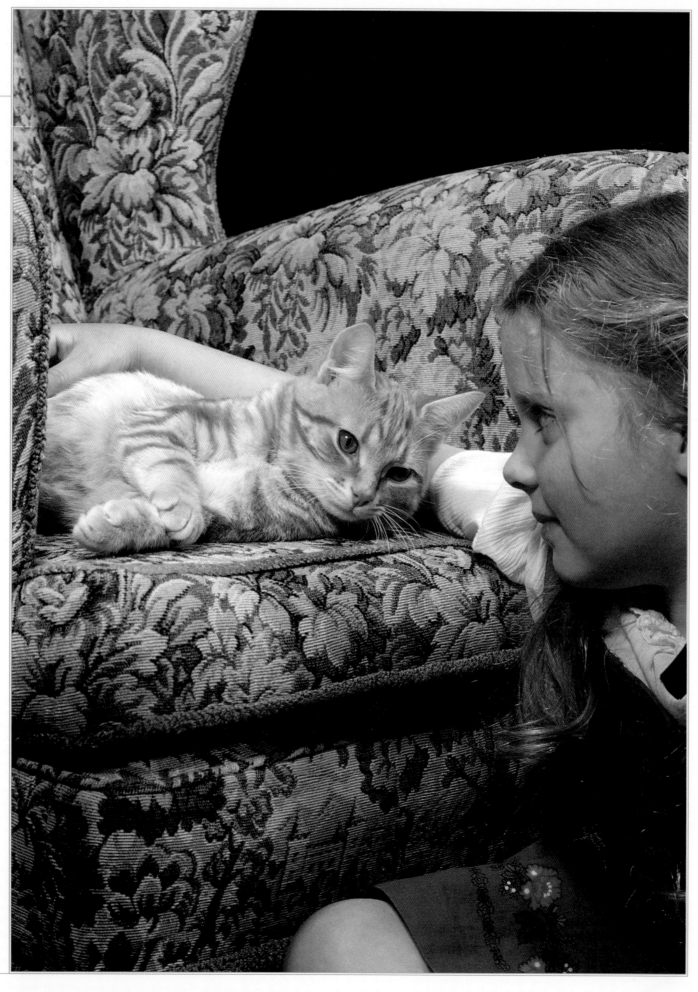

Creating the Right Environment

The domestic life is one in which a pet cat can feel secure in the knowledge of where the next meal is coming from. If you also provide an exciting and stimulating environment in which it can rest comfortably and where there are opportunities to climb and play, your cat will be a well-adjusted and rewarding companion. The financial outlay of buying the right equipment for your cat may seem high, but it is the first step in ensuring it leads a contented life.

✦ FACING PAGE
Cats may be independent and perfectly able to survive without humans, but as this ginger cat shows, they adapt well to a warm home and loving care.

✦ LEFT
A non-pedigreed cat sports his new flea collar.

SETTLING IN

Acquiring a cat should not be contemplated on a whim but with an awareness of the animal's continuing needs throughout its life in your home. Thoughtful preparation and planning before a new cat arrives is essential if the transition between old home and new is to be stress-free for both you and your pet. A cat needs time and space in which to adjust, and will settle down more easily, too, if all the right equipment is there when it arrives.

FORWARD PLANNING

This will be a new and strange environment for your cat, so before you collect it, check its diet with the breeder or cattery so that you know what it likes to eat and drink and can have some food ready.

The journey itself may be the first time in a kitten's short life that it has no other feline company. Even an older cat can be disorientated. While

travelling, talk to the animal in a calm voice. Do not be tempted to let it out of its carrier (in a car, for example) unless you have a companion with you who can restrain it.

THE ARRIVAL

A new arrival is a novelty and family and friends will want to be introduced, to stroke and play with the cat, especially if it is a kitten. This exciting time makes particular demands on

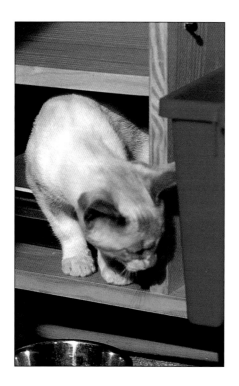

◆ TOP
The first sortie in the new home. The cage should be kept to hand so that the kittens can be put back in it until they become used to their new environment, and any other animals in the home can be surveyed from the safety of the pen.

◆ ABOVE
A young ginger cat has settled happily in the cat basket. A favourite blanket brought with it from its first home is an additional comfort.

◆ LEFT
A Siamese half-breed kitten explores the new home. It is important to let kittens explore in their own time, but supervision is advisable in case they become stuck or locked in a cupboard.

EQUIPMENT CHECKLIST

Not all the following are essential; those that are, are in heavy type.

- ◆ **bed and bedding**
- ◆ **litter and litter tray (pan)**
- ◆ **2 food bowls**
- ◆ **water bowl**
- ◆ **carrier**
- ◆ collar
- ◆ harness and lead
- ◆ identity tag
- ◆ cat flap

◆ RIGHT
Gradual, supervised
introductions over
the course of a few
weeks have enabled
this Irish Wolfhound
and Chinchilla to
feel at ease with each
other. However, such
close proximity
would not be
advisable with a
pet mouse!

◆ BELOW RIGHT
Kittens will quickly
seek out the most
comfortable places to
relax; if you do not
want them in your
bed, you need to
keep the door shut!

children who, without realizing the implications, may treat the new animal like a toy. However, try to make sure there are not many people around when the new arrival is introduced. It is tempting to rush straight into the living room and let the cat out of the carrier. Instead, take it immediately to where its litter tray (pan), sleeping space, food and water bowls are going to be permanently positioned. Such items are part of a familiar routine, which will be comforting. A drink and a little food may be all that is wanted.

EXTENDING TERRITORY

A kitten will want to explore and take in all the new sensory experiences of this new environment. It must be allowed to do this in its own time, and if that means that it wants to scurry about under a kitchen cupboard, out of sight, so be it. Eventually it will emerge and continue its exploration. Allow the kitten to do this at leisure. However, supervision is wise, in case it becomes locked in a cupboard or stuck on a high shelf. Handle the cat calmly and gently. Over-enthusiastic handling

can be very disorientating and may bring out the defence mechanisms. Being bitten or scratched does not endear anyone to a new pet, but from the kitten's point of view it was probably justified. By all means stroke the cat as it passes and talk to it. The reassurance of the human voice helps bridge the gap between old and new

homes. When a new cat is tired, it will probably find its bed on its own and it should be left to sleep undisturbed. Cats and kittens sleep more than any other mammal on a daily basis and, for a kitten, adequate sleep maintains and encourages the assimilation of food and enhances correct growth.

If you already have another cat or a dog, confine the new arrival to a small area at first – or even a cage – so that it can get used to where its food, water and litter are in peace, and the animals can adjust to one another in their own time. A cage in the kitchen or living room will provide security for the new arrival and quickly allow it to adjust to any other animals in the household and vice versa.

If you have a baby in the house, it is a good idea to put a cat net over the pram or cot. A cat is unlikely to harm the baby, but could be attracted to a warm, sleeping body and may want to curl up alongside it.

HANDLING AND HOLDING YOUR CAT

If you watch a mother cat, you will see how she picks up a tiny kitten by taking hold of the loose skin at the back of the neck and gently lifting. The kitten then demonstrates one of its inborn reflexes, which is to curl up into an apparently lifeless ball. It will not move until its mother puts it down. This loose skin, which becomes far less apparent as the kitten grows, is the scruff or nap. The action of picking up a cat in such a way is called scruffing. While it is possible to lift your cat in this way, scruffing should normally only be considered if absolutely necessary – if instant control is required, for example, when the cat is at the veterinary surgery. For less flexible adult cats especially, it can be an unnerving experience, particularly as they freeze when scruffed.

It is far better to pick up your kitten or cat by placing one hand under the chest, supporting the

backside with the other hand and then lifting. In this way the animal feels completely secure, with no limbs left dangling. This total support technique is essential if you are holding the cat for any length of time. As you and your cat become more confident, you can try different holds. Avoid tucking

the cat under your arm with its body, back legs and tail dangling like a ragdoll. This leaves most of its weight unsupported and puts a great strain on the internal organs. Many cats do not like being held for too long, and should be gently let down if they start to wriggle.

◆ RIGHT
Avoid surprising the cat when you are about to lift it. When it is relaxed, support the top of the hind legs with one hand and the chest with the other.

◆ FAR RIGHT
When holding or carrying a cat, keep the back end and legs supported. If the cat starts to wriggle, let it down gently; never force it to be held against its will, unless it is necessary.

BEDS AND BEDDING

During the initial settling-in period, a new kitten or cat should be able to settle down within easy reach of both litter tray (pan) and water. A simple cardboard box placed in a draught-proof spot with an old pillow and blanket is ideal. Then, if there are accidents, or if the cat's bedding becomes parasite-infested, everything can be burnt and little is lost.

Acrylic bedding is widely available, hygienic and easily laundered. Woollen materials, particularly if knitted, are not suitable as claws may become caught. Some cats seem also to be addicted to wool-sucking and chewing and this can cause congestion in the throat or digestive system.

Once the new arrival has settled in, you may want to provide a permanent bed. This can be made of wicker, moulded plastic or padded fabric, but it must be easy to wash and disinfect. Any bedding should be changed regularly. Very soon a collection of cushion beds, old jumpers, carpet-covered houses and other oddities will be adopted. Place these strategically where the cat likes to sleep at different times of the day.

◆ ABOVE
A cat is not fussy about the design of its bed. The advantage of a cardboard box is that if it becomes soiled or worn out, it can be easily replaced.

◆ LEFT
The owner's bed is often a favourite spot, especially if it has comfortable quilts and cushions.

◆ LEFT AND RIGHT
There is now such a range of pet beds available that you can choose one to match your decor. Whether you go for an enclosed, draughtproof and portable model or an open version, the easy-to-wash factor is the most important consideration.

LITTER AND LITTER TRAY (PAN)

A kitten or cat needs access to a litter tray (pan) if it is not able to go outside when it wants to. The tray may become redundant once a kitten is fully immunized and has learnt to use its cat flap into the garden, although it is preferable to encourage your cat to stay in at night. Even when very young, kittens are inherently clean and will not soil their bed. If a cage or crate is being used during the settling-in period, it should be large enough to contain a litter tray.

There is a wide range of products available, from basic plastic trays to covered models with entrance flaps and filters to minimize odour. The key

◆ LEFT
The most important consideration when buying a litter tray (pan) is that it should be easy to clean. Use a scoop to remove faeces independently, rather than changing all the litter in the tray every time.

point about litter trays is that they must be easy to clean, and tough enough to withstand frequent washing and disinfecting. They should also be in a position that is easy to clean. Toxoplasmosis is an infection that can

scrape the litter over any faeces deposited, which is does instinctively. Sawdust, woodshavings, cinders, ash and newspapers are not advised; nor are some pine-wood products that can be irritants.

◆ BELOW
The ultimate litter tray (pan) is not only draughtproof and private for the coy cat, but helps contain odours.

be shed in a cat's faeces without the cat showing any signs of disease. It is, however, a hazard to humans, especially pregnant women. Disposal of faeces less than 24 hours after passing and regular cleaning of litter trays with plenty of water and detergent is effective in the control of toxoplasmosis. Some household products contain ingredients, which, although fine for use in the home, can be toxic to cats. The staff at your vet's should be able to advise on these.

LITTER OPTIONS
The various litter products available should be acceptable to the cat, reduce odour and absorb urine. It should also be easy for the cat to

◆ ABOVE, LEFT TO RIGHT
Clay, wood and paper-based litters: some are highly absorbent, others are superfine and form clumps when wet.

◆ ABOVE
Kittens are instinctively clean. This feral kitten was abandoned by its mother and when a litter tray (pan) was provided, automatically began to use it after being shown it once.

FEEDING EQUIPMENT

If you already have perfectly suitable dishes, special purchases may not be necessary. The most practical choices are made of hard plastic, ceramic or stainless steel. All equipment should be easy to clean and disinfect. Discard cracked or chipped ceramic bowls, as germs may be harboured in the cracks. Once any container, new or old, has been allotted to the cat, it should not be used for anything else. Many people feed their cats in the kitchen; if there are dogs around, it is also likely that the cat is fed on a

TOXOPLASMOSIS

Toxoplasmosis affects many animals but cats are the only ones that shed the parasite in their faeces. This only happens for a short time after the cat has become infected and the faeces are only infectious after 24 hours or more. In most cases there are no visible signs of disease or illness in the cat. The infection is carried in the cat's faeces and in 24–48 hours can pass on to humans. Unless their immune system is not functioning properly, humans contracting the infection are unlikely to become ill, but if a pregnant woman is infected, there is a 40 per cent chance that her baby will also be infected. Of these infected babies, 15 per cent may spontaneously abort or acquire some abnormality.

◆ Wear gloves when gardening in an area frequented by cats

◆ Cover children's play areas, such as sand-pits, when not in use

◆ Empty litter trays (pans) on a daily basis and clean regularly with plenty of water and detergent

◆ Use a separate set of feeding equipment for the cat and do not use it for humans; clean regularly

◆ ABOVE, LEFT TO RIGHT FROM TOP LEFT
The cutlery for serving the cat should be exclusively for this purpose; plastic lids to cover unfinished tins prevent the food from drying up and the smell from spreading; a simple plastic bowl; a metal bowl; a plastic combined water and food bowl; an automatic feeder.

working surface. In either case it is especially important to maintain strict standards of hygiene to guard against the risk of toxoplasmosis (see box). The feeding area must be easy to clean and disinfect regularly. This is also important for the cat because it has a highly developed sense of smell and will reject food that has become tainted and hardened. For the same reasons, put down fresh water at least once a day. A closed-off eating area is advisable if you have crawling babies or toddlers.

For the busy owner whose lifestyle makes feeding the cat at regular times uncertain, automatic food bowls with timer switches are available. The cover automatically lifts to reveal food at pre-set times. A water bowl is kept topped up with water from a reservoir, but you do need to remember to change the reservoir frequently.

◆ RIGHT
It is more hygienic to put your cat's food on the floor rather than on a working surface where food is prepared for humans.

CARRIERS

It is essential to buy, rather than borrow, a cat carrier. You will need it not only to bring the cat or kitten home, but also for visits to the veterinary surgery – and anywhere else for that matter. Any visit to the vet will quickly reveal that very many owners have great faith in their pets' ability not to escape! They arrive with all sorts of contraptions for carrying their cats; sometimes with nothing at all to restrain an animal which may be in pain, very frightened and invariably highly stressed.

SIZE CONSIDERATIONS
Do not be seduced into buying a sweet, kitten-sized carrier; consider the future and purchase accordingly. That

✦ **ABOVE**
Large cat carriers provide plenty of room for your cat and can double up as pens for the settling-in period. They are, however, awkward to carry.

✦ **LEFT**
A top-loading wicker basket which could double as the cat's permanent bed.

cute little fur-ball is going to turn into a considerably larger adult. A carrier of around 30cm x 30cm x 55cm (12in x 12in x 22in) should last into the cat's adulthood. For an extra-large male, it might be wise to go to the next size up. Cats prefer to be in a fairly snug environment if they are experiencing a rare and disturbing event such as travelling, but they do need to be able to turn around and stretch out a little. They also like to be able to see out so that they feel a little less trapped.

If the journey is going to be a long one (over an hour or two), have a carrier that can take a small litter tray (pan) as well as clip-on water and food bowls. However, if you are likely to have to carry the cat very far, for example, when attending shows, remember the larger the carrier, the more awkward it is to carry. Strained shoulders and backs are not uncommon among exhibitors.

◆ BELOW
An easy-to-clean plastic container that might cause loading and unloading difficulties.

◆ BELOW
A collapsible cardboard carrier that can be dispensed with after being used to carry an infectious animal.

WHAT IS AVAILABLE

Basic cardboard carriers, preferably coated with plastic, are bought flatpacked, and, when assembled, are suitable for transporting a sick and possibly infectious animal, as they are inexpensive and can be burnt after use. However, they are not suitable for more regular use as they cannot be cleaned and disinfected effectively, and are not durable. Traditionalists choose wickerwork baskets, which come in various shapes, and usually have leather straps and a handle. These are attractive and could double as the cat's permanent sleeping quarters – at least the cat would be less likely to panic if travelling in its own bed.

Openwork wire baskets, especially with the wire covered with white plastic, have veterinary approval because they are so easy to disinfect and the cat is easily visible. The top opening is secured by a separate rod pushed through rigid loops. Moulded plastic carriers with strategically placed ventilation holes are available in a great range of designs, are easy to dismantle for thorough cleaning, and

reassembling is no problem either. Clear moulded plastic (Perspex) carriers with airholes are a less worthwhile investment as the plastic tends to crack and degrade over time. If carried in sunlight, its occupant can quickly overheat.

The most practical designs are those with top access; they are less stressful both for cat and handler. The

cat can be grasped from above and removed without a struggle. With a front-loading carrier, the often frightened animal has to be recovered from the back of a tunnel. It can also be difficult to put the cat back inside.

◆ BELOW
If you want your cat carrier to look distinctive or decorative, you could paint it with an appropriate design.

COLLARS, HARNESSES AND LEADS

A collar is not necessarily merely decorative. A tag may be attached to it so that the cat can be identified if it gets lost or injured. An identity tag may be a simple engraved disc or a screw-topped cylinder containing a roll of paper with the cat's name, owner's address and telephone number, and sometimes the vet's emergency number. Magnetic tags that allow your cat exclusive entry to its cat flap can also be fitted on collars.

Most collars come with a bell which rings when the cat moves and will reduce the death toll among garden birds and other potential hunting targets. Some collars are impregnated with an anti-flea substance, but keep a careful check on your cat when you first put one on it, as they can cause an allergic reaction. Signs of irritation around the neck or eyes are the main indications of allergy. A flea collar should never be combined with any other form of flea control.

Collars have two main disadvantages. If worn continuously, as they should be if they are carrying any form of identification, they will damage the fur around the neck,

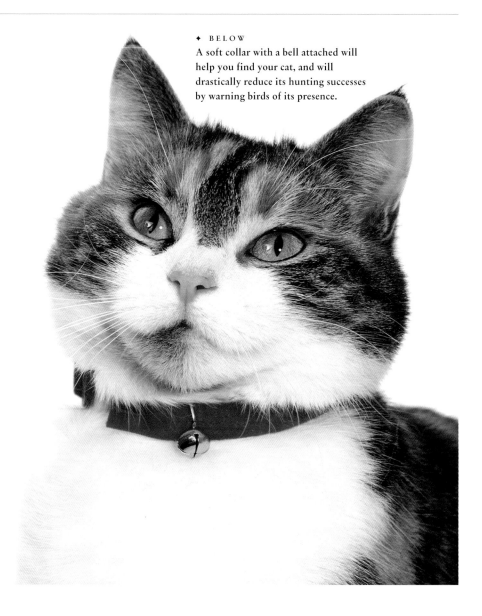

◆ BELOW
A soft collar with a bell attached will help you find your cat, and will drastically reduce its hunting successes by warning birds of its presence.

◆ ABOVE
A soft, padded flea collar with a bell and an elastic section. Flea collars should only be used on cats over six months old. They may cause an allergic reaction in some cats.

◆ ABOVE
A soft leather collar with the all-important elastic section. Any collar you buy should have this, for if the collar is caught the elastic will stretch, allowing the cat to escape unharmed.

◆ ABOVE
Fabric collars, which can be cut to size without fraying, are useful for kittens and small cats. They are cheap enough to be changed regularly, or even to have a selection of different colours.

especially that of longhaired cats. This can be unsightly and is considered unacceptable by many exhibitors; although most show judges realize the reason for any marks around the neck, they may still penalize the cat. Secondly, there is always the fear that the collar can become caught when the cat is hunting in trees or shrubs. However, if it is made of soft leather, suede, or soft fabric and has an elasticated insert, this will stretch if the collar catches, and the cat will be able to free itself. The collar should always be adjusted so that it will slip over the cat's head in an emergency, but not loose enough to allow the front leg to slip through and the collar to lodge under the armpit, which could cause injury.

GOING FOR A WALK

Cat leads are only necessary if you intend to take your cat for walks or if you are taking it to a strange house and need to keep it under control. Some cats actively enjoy this, particularly Siamese. It is not unusual to see this breed travelling on public transport on a lead. However, most cats are naturally resistant to wearing any such controlling apparatus and will fight against it, especially if they become frightened. To take them on a bus or train on a lead rather than in a carrier is foolhardy under any

circumstances. If the cat panics, it could either become tangled and hurt itself, or escape. If a lead is worn on a more suitable outing, it should be no more than 1m (3ft) long, and have a fitted harness rather than a collar for attachment. This not only allows more control and comfort, but is more secure. Cats are great escapologists, however, and even the most carefully fitted harness may prove insecure.

Introduce your cat to a harness and lead as early as possible. Put the harness on first by itself, and just for a short time each day. After you have done this for a few days, attach the lead for a short time, several days running, but just leave it trailing. When the cat seems relaxed about the lead, try walking it, first indoors for brief spells, then in the garden, and then in a street where the cat can get used to traffic and people, but do not overdo it!

◆ LEFT
Magnetic tags double as a means of identity and a "key" to enable the wearer to go through its cat flap.

◆ BELOW
Some oriental cats appear to enjoy going for walks, but they need to be familiarized with a collar or harness and lead from an early age.

◆ LEFT
Identity tags can be simple metal discs engraved with the owner's name and telephone number, or an information-packed barrel containing the owner's address and the vet's address and emergency telephone number.

EXTRAS AND TOYS

Play for a young cat is just as essential for its well-being as it is for a human child. It is particularly important for the owner to play with the cat if it is the only one in the household. Through play, muscles are exercised and conditioned, the brain is kept alert and the eyes bright. And if the owner joins in, it strengthens the bond between the feline and its adopted human family.

At the very least your cat should have a scratching post, which it can be encouraged to use instead of the furniture and soft furnishings. A cat will naturally use surfaces such as the bark of a tree to sharpen and control the length of its claws – they are its main means of defence, and also provide grip when climbing. You can make an indoor scratching post yourself by binding a stout fence post with heavy-duty sisal string or cotton rope, and attaching it to a suitable base. A strip of old carpet is an alternative, but this is not as effective for the cat, as it frays quickly, creates a great deal of fluff, and needs to be

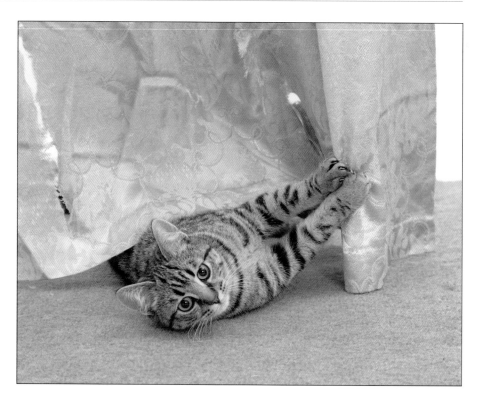

renewed regularly. If you do not mind your cat equipment taking over the home, feline climbing frames of varying size and complexity are readily available. Some are over 2m (6ft) high, with circular supports covered in sisal rope, carpet-covered perches, houses and barrels. They are likely to be found at cat shows, or through advertisements in specialist cat magazines and larger pet stores.

PLAY WITH A PURPOSE

A cat's play is orientated to the hunting process. When a cat swoops after a leaf in autumn, that leaf is an imaginary bird. The ping-pong ball just visible behind a chair leg is a mouse to be stalked, pounced upon and batted around. The screwed-up paper hurled into the air, caught and thrown away to be chased and sent flying again, is being

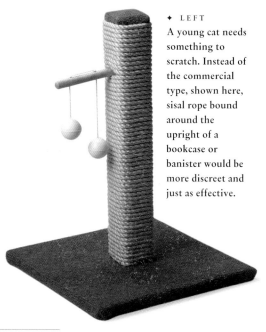

◆ LEFT
A young cat needs something to scratch. Instead of the commercial type, shown here, sisal rope bound around the upright of a bookcase or banister would be more discreet and just as effective.

◆ ABOVE
Being ten months old does not mean that this youngster has grown out of shredding curtains for fun.

◆ BELOW
Kittens enjoy playing with someone, especially if they are an only cat; they will soon become bored playing on their own with a ball.

◆ LEFT
The perfect combination for a family cat –
company, care, attention, and a game that seems
to be tailor-made for cats. Be careful of any
electrical connections, though.

◆ ABOVE
Cats are nature's most efficient predators: a
fabric mouse filled with delectable catnip may
not last long in the grip of this young Ocicat.

hunted. Even in an apparently sterile
environment, a cat will find a scrap of
paper, a lost button, or a shadow to
play with. However, do be careful of
everyday household objects like the
odd button or needle and thread.
Swallowed thread can do even more
damage than a needle as it cheesewires
its way through the bowel.

Do check that any cat toys you buy
are reasonably solid. Some cheap
imported toys may have small plastic
bits that could fall off and be
swallowed. Some plastic materials that
are safe for children can be toxic to
cats. All that is needed can be found in
the home: paper scrunched into a ball
and thrown by the owner for retrieval
up and down the stairs; a paper
"butterfly" tied to a piece of string
and dragged around for the cat to
chase, or suspended from the back of
a chair to bat. Some cats are
particularly fond of hide-and-seek.
For group play, nothing is better than
the great game of the ping-pong ball
rolled around the carpet between
family members and friends, and
pursued by your cat.

◆ BELOW
A clockwork mouse is a poor
substitute for the real thing, as
it has to be wound up, but it is
less messy for
the owner.

◆ RIGHT
You will probably need a continuing
supply of replacement balls as they are
constantly being batted out of sight.

◆ RIGHT
Here's a soft, friendly chap to dig your claws
into. Let's hope the bear's eyes are well secured
so that the kitten does not swallow them.

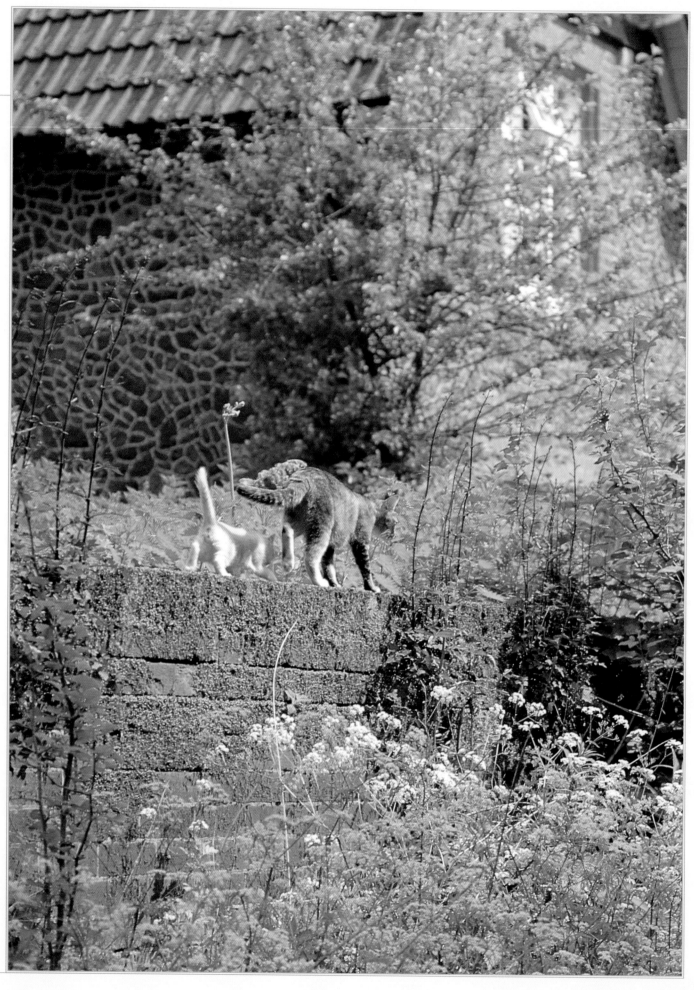

Care at Home and Away

A cat instinctively knows its physical limits; it can also, through learned behaviour and training, avoid potentially dangerous situations. The wise owner strikes a balance between giving the cat the freedom it needs, being aware of the dangers it could face, and protecting it from them.

◆ FACING PAGE
A mother introduces one of her
kittens to the outside world. She will
teach it survival and hunting skills.

◆ ABOVE
A well-cared-for ginger and white
non-pedigree is completely relaxed
at home and away.

CONTROLLING A CAT'S TERRITORY

If you live in an apartment block or in a busy urban environment, or your cat is frail or a valuable pedigree, it is perfectly feasible – and acceptable to most cats – to keep it indoors all the time. In some parts of the United States, vets actively recommend this for cats in urban environments.

Because of the balanced pet foods now available, modern cats do not need to go out to supplement their diet by hunting. Outdoor exercise is also unnecessary, as long as the owner provides toys and plays with the cat.

Although cats are nocturnal by nature, it is really unwise to allow much-loved pets to stay out at night. Train them to stay in from an early age and make sure there is always a clean litter tray (pan) available. This training also ensures that they are equally happy if kept indoors for long periods.

The outdoor cat's tendency to roam and exposure to the dangers of traffic, fighting and infection from other cats, can be reduced at a snip – that is, by being neutered (altered). The sex-drive of a calling queen or an active

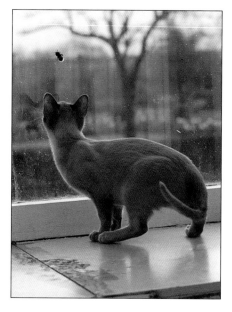

✦ ABOVE
A Burmese is attracted to the outside world. Some cats are freedom-loving and do not like being kept indoors.

✦ RIGHT
A ginger kitten has taken over the best armchair. An indoor cat needs plenty of toys and active input from its owner if it is not to become bored and substitute the upholstery for a tree.

THE MAKING OF AN INDOOR CAT

The consultant, a breeder of Maine Coon Cats, does not let his cats out until they are well over six months old – two to three months after they have been neutered (altered). The cats are trained to litter trays (pans) and so, when they are eventually let out, it is not long before they rush back in to use their usual toilet facilities. Because they are neutered (altered), their hunting and roaming instinct is greatly curtailed and they seldom stray beyond their familiar garden.

✦ LEFT
A Persian has the comfort-loving temperament suited to an indoor life, and its long coat is easier to care for inside.

tom cat will override any considerations for road safety. The unneutered male cat can hunt over an area of about 11km (7 miles). His desexed counterparts will probably exercise territorial rights over maybe 200m (240 yards) at most.

DANGERS IN THE HOME

There are dangers even for the cat that is kept indoors all the time. Those who live in high-rise buildings should erect netting across open windows and around balconies. The defences can be camouflaged by plants. Even within the house, cats should be allowed access to heights only if they are considered safe. A specific danger area is a staircase with openwork bannisters from which a kitten could launch itself into space – not necessarily landing on its feet. Kittens should be supervised as they explore.

THE ALLURE OF MACHINES

The warmth, the smells and the movement of washing and drying machines attract a cat's attention. Always make sure that the appliance's doors are kept closed when not in use. Before you turn the machine on, check that there is no cat curled inside. The smell of food in a fridge is also enticing. At least if it were to be inadvertently incarcerated, a cat would survive there for some time, as long as there was sufficient air available. It would not, however, survive for long in a freezer. Fifteen minutes would probably be long enough to cause irreversible hypothermia.

PLAYING WITH FIRE

Burns and scalds sustained by cats exploring the source of interesting food smells are not unusual and are sometimes very severe. Cats have been known to dance across the hot rings of an electric cooker, badly damaging their paws.

Electric cables are potential playthings, so make sure no wires are loose or exposed, and if you spot your cat chewing them, conceal the cables beneath a carpet, or cover them with a catproof material such as thick, loose rubber or plastic tubing. A cat will nose around drawers and boxes packed with interesting oddments – but here too, are potential dangers such as pins and paper clips. Tasty, pingy elastic bands may be fun to pick at and chew, but could cause choking and suffocation, and the same goes for lengths of wool or cotton, or plastic film. Cats are also attracted to olives, the stones of which are just the right size to become stuck in a feline throat. Open fireplaces should always be guarded, even when a fire is not lit, for cats like climbing up chimneys and may become stuck or break a limb, or at the very least emerge soot-covered. Electric and gas fires can be equally dangerous. One cat owner was faced with a fire in her living room and some very frightened kittens, after the combined weight of the litter of kittens toppled a highly flammable chair against the bars of a gas fire.

◆ LEFT
A very cosy scene for mother and kitten – however, open fires should always be kept guarded unless you are in the room to keep an eye on your cat.

◆ ABOVE
The washing machine has just been turned off and is still warm, making it a possible spot to curl up in for an undisturbed sleep.

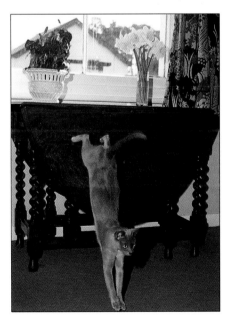

◆ ABOVE
The deliberate leap from the table is well within this cat's capability, but a kitten could hurt itself if it fell or jumped from such a height.

ACCESS TO THE OUTSIDE WORLD

It always used to be common practice to put the house cat out at night, so that it could carry out its rodent extermination duties, and to avoid mess in the house. Effective rodent control and the availability of litter trays (pans) have made this unnecessary. Now a cat's freedom is more likely to be dependent upon human work patterns. However, unless you have pedigreed cats which you keep for exhibition and show, or your living space necessitates an indoor lifestyle, you can allow your pet various degrees of access to the outside world.

Some cats automatically confine their territories to the back garden. Others may develop an awareness of the traffic in their area, and avoid rush hours, for example. However, it is difficult to be sure of their abilities, and even quiet streets can be dangerous because of the occasional,

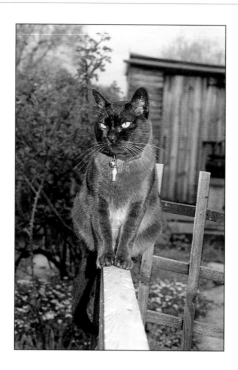

unexpected vehicle. For these reasons, and the risks of territorial fighting and exposure to infection, it is worth exercising some form of control over your cat's freedom to roam.

♦ ABOVE
A Brown Burmese selects a high vantage point from which to survey the surrounding territory.

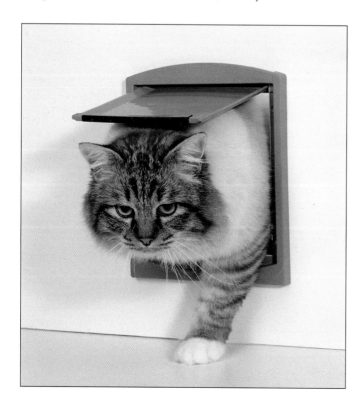

♦ LEFT
A cat will soon learn to use its cat flap with confidence. The flap swings shut when the cat has passed through.

CAT FLAPS

Cat flaps are cat-sized windows that are fitted about 15cm (6in) from the base of a door. The most practical design is one that is gravity-loaded so that the door automatically closes after entry or exit, and with a clear plastic window so that the cat can look through it before venturing outside.

Flaps are a boon to the indoor/outdoor cat that is not afraid of operating the flap and whose owners are not always home to obey the cat's every whim. They allow both cat and owner a degree of independence from each other. The main disadvantage of cat flaps, particularly when there is no such feline control, is that neighbours or feral cats will soon learn to use them, particularly if delicious food is known to be available on the other side of the flap. This could lead to disease or infection being brought into the home, or territorial fights, or both. One way of overcoming this is to have an electronically operated flap that allows entry only to cats wearing the appropriate collar and gadgetry – usually in the form of a magnetic tag that doubles as an identity tag.

Alternatively, you can allow your cat limited freedom, and, for example, lock the flap at night when you are unable to keep an eye on unwanted visitors. It is useful to buy a flap that can be locked to prevent your cat from going out at certain times, or other cats from coming in. Your cat will soon become used to whatever routine you set.

When you introduce your cat to the cat flap, spend some time encouraging it with your voice and showing it how the door works. Put the cat on one side and call encouragingly from the

A tom cat prepares for his nocturnal prowl.
Many of the small rodents that cats hunt are
active as night falls, and this also seems to be a
prime time to look for a mate.

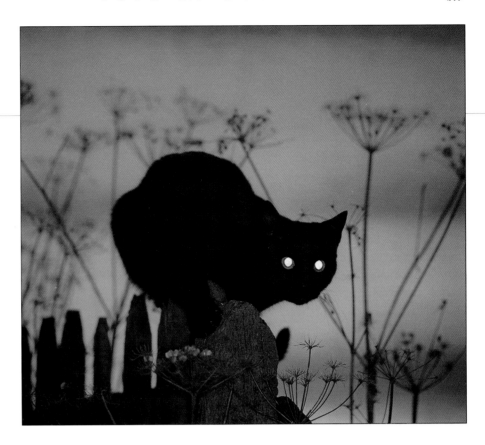

other. After a few tries, it will know
exactly what to do by itself. However,
it is not unusual for some cats to
steadfastly refuse to use a flap –
particularly if the flap was introduced
after the cat. The same goes for flaps
on covered litter trays (pans).

OUTDOOR CONFINEMENT

Indoor living can be safely
supplemented by a secure outdoor
area. Areas of a garden can be fenced
in with wire or plastic mesh like a fruit
cage, or a purpose-built shed or pen
can be provided. Climbing plants can
be trained to cover the sides to soften
the appearance, but take advice on
which plants to choose – some are
poisonous to cats.

A pen can be constructed in the
garden or as an extension to the house
(with access via a cat flap). It should
be sturdy in structure with wire or
plastic mesh stretched between a solid
wood frame, and roofed. Features

could include a covered shelter and an
outdoor play area with logs, shelves
and playthings to keep the cats amused.
Such pens are commercially available.
In extreme cases, or with very small
areas, whole gardens are secured
around the perimeter to prevent cats
from escaping and, more importantly,

other cats from getting in. You can
make a framework of stout posts to a
height of say 3m (9ft) and attach wire
netting between them. If the netting is
loosely fitted the cat will not be able
to climb up it and there will be no need
to roof in the top. The base of the wire
should be buried or well secured.

✦ ABOVE
A lithe hunter like this Brown Burmese will be
a joy to watch in your garden.

✦ RIGHT
Cats are often attracted to the shelter and
warmth offered by parked cars, so always check
beneath your car before you drive away.

✦ FAR RIGHT
Cats enjoy fresh air and sunshine from the
safety of an outside pen.

IN THE GARDEN

To watch a cat move and play in a garden is a source of delight, but there are dangers. Cats can swim, but are not generally renowned for their ability in this area, and there are cases of accidental drowning each year. The simple solution in the case of a garden pond, stream or swimming pool, is to cover the water with very fine mesh or to erect a barrier to make the area inaccessible to the cat.

Cats do have a wonderful righting ability which enables them to almost invariably land on their feet when falling from a height. However, vets regularly see cats that have been badly injured as a result of falls. If a cat lands on an unyielding surface, it is likely to injure itself if the fall is more than 3–4m (9–12ft), which is equivalent in height to the first storey of a house. The same applies if they fall out of trees. The most common problem with cats climbing is that they become absorbed in either hunting or exploring and end up on a branch too small to turn around on and escape.

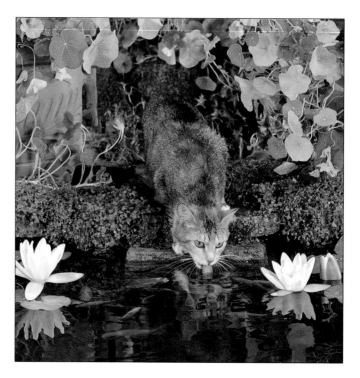

This is when the rescue services are called in. Discourage habitual climbers by placing wire netting around the base of favourite or particularly dangerous trees. However, the determined feline may just look for another tree.

◆ LEFT
When maturity and wisdom have taken the place of adventure and curiosity, a garden can be a great place for sunning and relaxation.

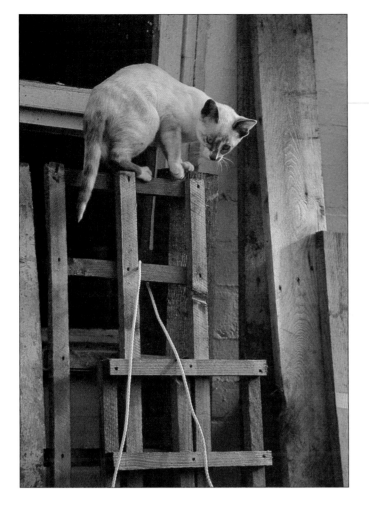

INSURANCE

Compare the cover and terms of several companies that specialize in animal insurance before you make your decision. The owner of a valuable cat may want to insure against loss, death or theft, in order to reclaim the cat's value. More general policies cushion the owner against the cost of veterinary bills in the event of accident or emergency, injury or disease, but do not cover initial injections, neutering or standard booster inoculations. The annual premium depends upon the level of cover selected and upon the insured animal's medical history. Deciding whether or not to insure is a matter of balancing what can be a fairly steep monthly or annual premium against your ability to pay any sudden, costly vet's bill. The alternative, as with any insurance cover, is to have your own contingency account to cover emergency expenses.

Cat breeders sometimes issue basic health insurance cover notes with kittens. Cover starts from the date of sale and is usually valid for six weeks. After that, the new owner can continue with the same policy or seek another one.

TRAPPED

Apart from harbouring dangerous substances, garden sheds and garages can become prisons from which there is no escape. A brief period of captivity will not do a cat too much harm. A cat can survive for 10–14 days without food and almost as long without water, provided the ambient temperature is not too high, but the resulting

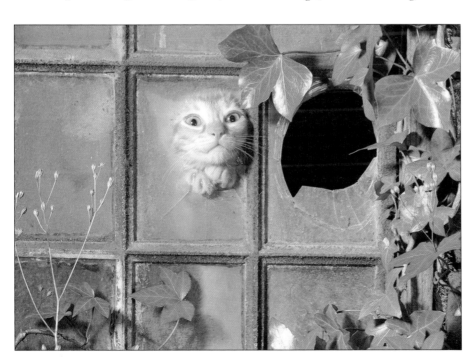

dehydration and starvation may have serious consequences for the proper functioning of kidneys and liver. Such a physically challenged cat is then prey to secondary infections it would normally easily shake off. If you have not seen your cat for a while, check in cellars, cupboards, tool sheds and garages, in case it is trapped. Before you go away, make sure your cat is there, and that a neighbour (or the person looking after the cat) has access to the house, and any sheds or garages.

♦ BELOW
A farm kitten has found a warm, sunny spot to
sit in. Let's hope there are no nasty nitrates or
rat poison lying around!

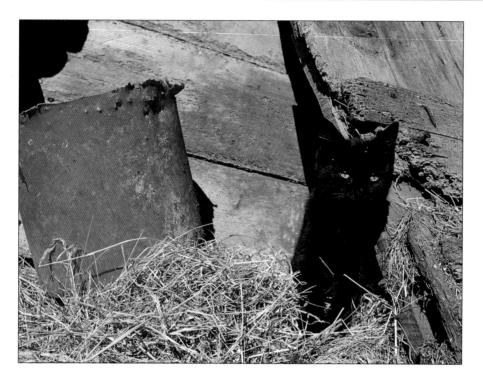

THE RISK OF POISONING

A cat enjoys exploring and takes an interest in dark, small places where danger can lurk in the form of toxic substances. A cat can occasionally be poisoned by eating or drinking poison, by indirect absorption from eating a poisoned animal, or, more commonly, by licking poison deposited on the fur or paw pads. Similarly, these substances can be absorbed through the skin itself, particularly through the paw pads.

It is vital to keep household cleaning agents in cupboards with catproof doors, and antifreezes and weedkillers safely locked away in garages and tool sheds. Always read the labels of such products carefully; if there are warnings of the danger of the contents to children, they are likely to be bad for your cat too. Although a cat is not likely to choose to drink a bottle of paint-stripper, it could knock

♦ BELOW
This terracotta pot looks safe enough – as long
as it does not topple over, and there are no
dangerous substances left inside.

♦ BELOW
A cat has taken over the greenhouse. It was
allergic to tomatoes, so the plants and all
potentially dangerous substances were removed
before the cat moved in.

over a bottle containing some. If a toxic substance is spilled on a surface where a cat is likely to tread, mop it up thoroughly. If you are decorating, keep the cat out of the room. Even the smell of modern decorating materials can affect some cats.

Some of the preparations used to keep garden pests at bay are particularly lethal, as they are spread around the garden. Your cat might eat the bird that ate the slug that took the slug pellet, or it just might lick its pads on to which a slug pellet has adhered. So check the contents of any weedkillers, slug bait or growth enhancers and opt for the environmentally friendly varieties. Even these may carry a warning

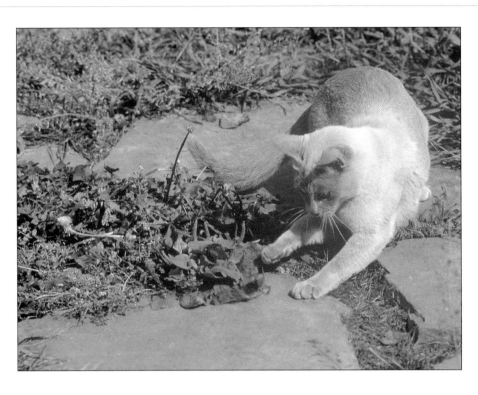

◆ ABOVE RIGHT
The mouse that this young cat is playing with could carry toxins picked up at an earlier point in the food chain.

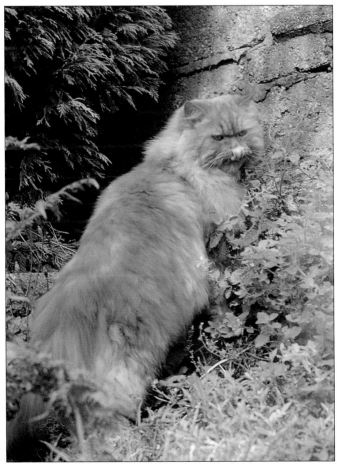

◆ RIGHT
A robust ginger non-pedigree is seeking out some greenstuff to supplement his diet. Most cats instinctively avoid potentially poisonous plants.

regarding domestic pets, and some cats have particular reactions to some substances that are safe for the majority, so keep alert.

Cats usually instinctively avoid the plants which are poisonous to them. However, indirect poisoning could possibly occur if the cat were to eat a bird or a small rodent that had fed on such a plant. Cats do eat grass and other herbage to provide minerals and vitamins, and to act as emetics to get rid of fur balls, for example. Outdoor cats are free to choose their own greenstuff and, because of their normally fastidious nature, seldom make mistakes by taking a mouthful of a toxic plant. Seeds of grasses that are beneficial to cats are marketed, and can be grown indoors. If you do have an indiscriminate plant chewer, avoid having plants that could be dangerous in the house and garden. A garden centre should be able to advise on what these are.

GOING AWAY

Most cats are probably happier to stay in their own homes when owners are away, and there are organizations that will arrange for people to move in and care for your pets. However, this service can be expensive if only one animal is involved. Most people arrange for friends, neighbours, or relatives to live in or to come in regularly to feed and check on the cat. This can sometimes present problems as cats are great individualists, and even if they appear friendly with the sitter when the owners are present may adopt a different view when they have left. In such a situation, a cat might become stressed and stray. It is wise to have a few practice runs and leave the cat for a few days before

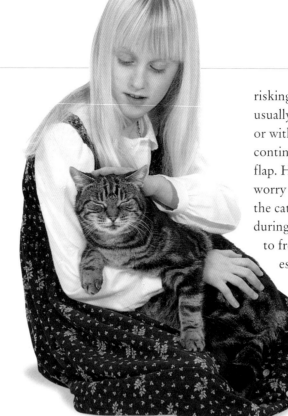

✦ ABOVE
Food, water and a clean litter tray (pan) are not all a cat wants when its owners are away. Cuddles and games are also important if your cat is not to feel lonely.

risking a two-week break. There is usually no problem with indoor cats, or with outdoor cats that are able to continue coming and going via a cat flap. However, this can be an added worry for the carer, who may prefer the cat flap to be securely locked during the owner's absence. Cats used to freedom might be very keen to escape if suddenly confined in this way. Do make sure, before you leave, that the person who is to look after your cat knows where the cat is and has the keys to all the places to which the cat might have access – the house, the garage, plus any outhouses. Always leave your contact telephone number, and the address and telephone number of your vet, including the emergency service. Discuss responsibilities before you go to ensure that what needs to be done is absolutely clear. Leave written instructions if necessary.

BOARDING OUT

If you decide not to have someone looking after your cat at home, ask your vet for approved local catteries (many veterinary practices have boarding facilities of their own), or ask friends for first-hand recommendations. Do make arrangements well in advance of your departure, as the best boarding catteries may be booked up for months ahead. It is a good idea to visit the cattery before booking to see if the environment and atmosphere will suit your cat. Most prefer you to make an appointment beforehand. There are also questions a boarding cattery

✦ LEFT
Being home alone while the owners are away does not present too much of a problem for this cat. It has the freedom of the house, a cat flap for access to outside, and a reliable neighbour to call in and feed it.

Points to check on your preliminary visit to a cattery:

✦ are there individual runs?

✦ are the runs and houses inside or outside, and are they are adequately heated?

✦ are the pens sheltered, clean and safely out of the reach of dogs if they are taken in too?

✦ are the beds and bedding disposed of or thoroughly disinfected for each new resident?

✦ are the feeding bowls sterilized between residents?

✦ do the staff seem happy, bright and animal-loving? Do they have any qualifications?

✦ is there plenty for your cat to watch?

✦ do the runs have appropriate sneeze gaps between them? Are the partitions impervious?

✦ are there climbing posts permanently available?

✦ how often are the cats visited during the day?

✦ are the kitchens clean?

✦ is there access to a vet at all times?

✦ ABOVE
This boarding cattery has outside pens. If you have an indoor cat, will it be happy and warm enough here?

✦ LEFT
On your preliminary visit to a cattery you could check other residents to see if they look contented.

owner will ask of you, most importantly whether the cat is in good health and has up-to-date vaccination status. The cattery should have details of your vet's name, address and telephone number, and your own contact address and telephone numbers while you are away. You will be asked for details of special dietary requirements for your cat, and will need to sign a consent form regarding appropriate treatment in the case of illness, and your acceptance of any necessary veterinary bills.

✦ RIGHT
Check there is enough sneezing distance between one pen and another, just in case one inmate develops an infection.

TRAVELLING TIPS

If you anticipate regular travelling with your cat – to shows, for example – it is worth introducing travelling at an early age. Any length of journey can be very stressful for a cat, and you should try to create as secure an environment as possible within the carrier. Some cats – especially Siamese – can complain loudly throughout a journey: they are distressed because they feel trapped. This can be very distracting for the driver. A vet can administer a tranquillizer, but this should be avoided if possible. Because of the stress factor, it is not advisable to subject a pregnant cat, or a nursing mother and young kittens to travelling.

If there is no room for a litter tray (pan), lay some form of absorbent padding – absorbent kitchen paper, or a baby's nappy (diaper) – on the base. Avoid newsprint, especially if you have a light-coloured cat whose fur might stain. Spread one of the cat's usual sleeping blankets or towels on top, and add a favourite toy.

✦ LEFT
A pedigreed cat is going off to a show. As it is travelling alone with the driver, the carrier will have to be firmly secured on the back seat of the car.

✦ BELOW LEFT
A Seal Point Siamese emerges from its lightproof and draughtproof container.

COMFORT IN TRANSIT

Seasoned cat show travellers suggest that the cat carrier should be placed as far away from the engine as possible, away from engine noise, and from direct blasts of dry air from heaters and fans. Some carriers have a specially designed cover to keep out light and draughts (drafts). Otherwise, on cold days, you can cover the carrier with a blanket or towel. Do make sure there are sufficient gaps for ventilation. In the early days of cat shows, owners would send their prize animals by train in such carefully sealed baskets that on occasions the cats arrived dead from suffocation.

BOOK AHEAD

Before booking a bus or coach journey, always contact the company you intend to travel with well in advance to check their regulations on the transportation of animals. Companies have different rules and it may not be possible for your cat to travel with you, if at all. In the United States, for instance, the Greyhound bus line does not permit pets. You will almost certainly have to pay a fare for your pet. Few companies consider them as hand baggage.

AIR TRAVEL

Commercial airlines have well-established regulations for the transportation of pets. These conform to International Air Transport Association (IATA) regulations. It is vital to contact the airline offices at least a month in advance of the travel date to ascertain requirements. You may be required to buy a carrier that has to be ordered by mail from a specialist supplier. In any event, the carrier should be of a strong, rigid material, stable and well-ventilated. There needs to be a handle for ease of carrying, and a door that can be locked to guard against anyone opening it. A

◆ ABOVE
A sturdy carrier suitable for an air journey has a ridge around it to guard against the ventilation holes becoming blocked.

label carrying the owner's name and address, together with instructions for any feeding or watering that might be necessary should be securely attached. If the journey is to be a long one, and the carrier is not big enough for a litter tray (pan), line the base with plenty of absorbent towelling or a disposable nappy (diaper).

Some airlines allow a cat in its carrier to stay with its owner in the passenger section. Usually, though, your cat will be housed with other animals booked on the flight in a special area of the hold which provides an environment with heat, light and air-conditioning, according to IATA regulations.

◆ LEFT
For short journeys – to the vet, for example – two cats are company for each other. On longer hauls, this would constitute overcrowding.

CHANGING COUNTRIES

It is not only top breeders who export their highly prized pedigreed cats and kittens to countries around the world. Retirement, career changes or even health considerations can prompt cat owners to move from one country to another, and if it is for any significant length of time, the cat goes too!

Arranging exportation first involves contact with the local animal health offices of the relevant government department – the Ministry of Agriculture, Fisheries and Food (MAFF) in the United Kingdom or the Department of Agriculture in the United States. This should be done as soon as possible and will provide essential information. You will need an export licence, and it is advisable to apply for this about four–six weeks in advance. This is due to the fact that

◆ LEFT
A cat in quarantine has a private shelf and plenty of room in which to run around.

◆ BELOW
So who is on holiday? This quarantine cattery is at Oahu, Hawaii.

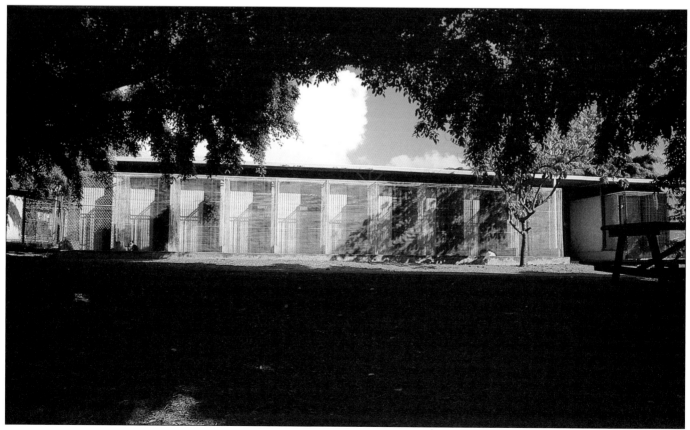

◆ BELOW
A show cat is not subjected to the strict
quarantine regulations still imposed in Britain,
as long as certain requirements are met.

vaccination against specific diseases is mandatory for a number of importing countries and has to be administered at a specific minimum time before import is allowed. Many countries receiving cats from the United Kingdom will insist upon the rabies vaccine having been administered at least 28 days prior to import. As the United Kingdom has been, to date, free of rabies, the rabies vaccine is only issued to authorized vets who are Local Veterinary Inspectors (LVI) of MAFF. The application must state details of both owner and animal, date, importing country and method of travel. A special order has to be raised for each individual dose and, in most cases, the injection still has to be given a clear 28 days before the animal leaves the country. In some cases, proof of vaccination against rabies (and other diseases, depending on the importing country) will be required before the issue of an export licence.

Paperwork is scrutinized carefully upon entry at immigration. Often, precise details of the departure date and time, the consignee's address, route and method of travel may be required on the import documents as well as on the rabies vaccine application order. The airline will give you precise details of the type of carrier in which the animal is to be sent, and what you should include in it for the journey.

Some countries insist on a period of quarantine to keep rabies out of rabies-free areas. In Britain, although the law is under review, there is still a statutory six months' quarantine before an imported pet cat may be released to its owners. Do carefully consider the effects on the cat of

such a long separation, and the expense involved. A quarantine kennels may want guarantees of a cat's fitness before accepting it, and may also require a male cat to be

◆ ABOVE
When your cat arrives in its new home, it will need a great deal of attention and to be kept indoors for a while.

neutered (altered). A nine-month-old Greek stray raised by an English family severed a nerve in its leg shortly before it was due to move to Britain. As well as the stress of the journey, it would have had to be neutered (altered) and its leg amputated, followed by six months' quarantine and a complete change of climate and environment. Fortunately, the Greek vet offered it a home.

IMPORT OF SHOW CATS

The British regulations have relaxed a little for animals intended for "trade" – which means show cats are included but not ordinary household pets. Such animals can be imported into Britain without undergoing quarantine, provided that stringent pre-entry requirements are met. These include vaccination against rabies, blood-testing to assess immunity, implantation of an identity microchip, and importation from a registered holder on whose premises the cat has either been born or been continuously resident for the previous six months.

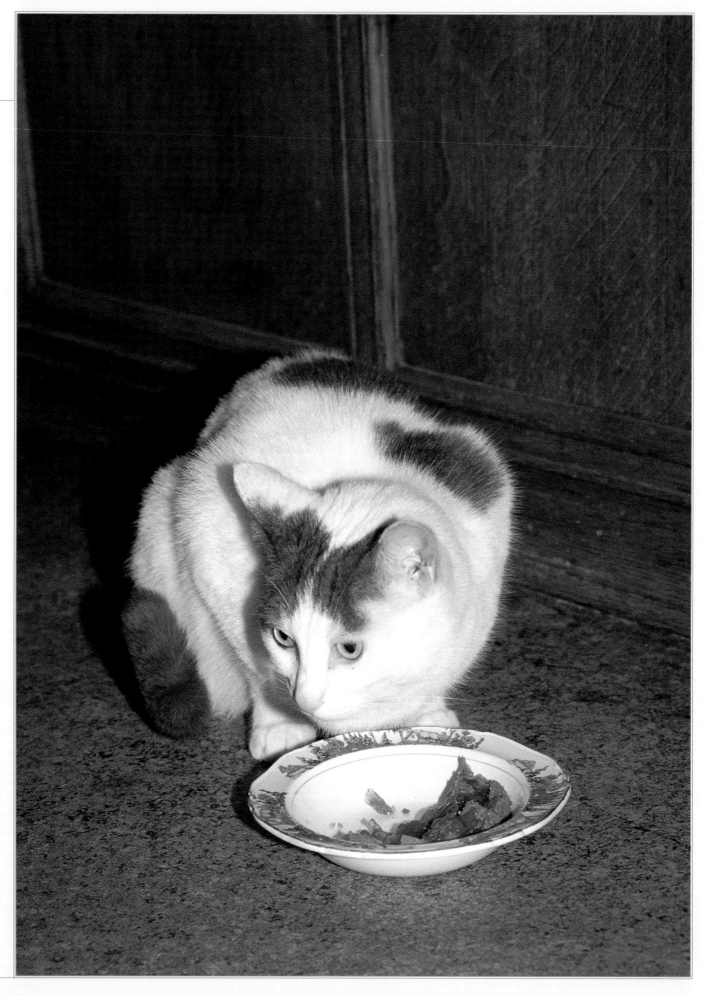

Nutrition and Feeding

If you give your cat a well-balanced diet, it will radiate good health. It will be contented, alert and active, with bright eyes, a glossy coat and a moist nose. Regular feeding and a variety of textures and flavours may also contribute to a contented and healthy cat.

◆ FACING PAGE
Dinner is served on a plate, but if the owner were to disappear, this cat would adapt to finding its own food in the wild.

◆ ABOVE
Two can be company when it comes to meal-times, as long as each cat obtains its fair share.

EATING HABITS

♦ BELOW
A cat stalks its prey, a pastime it enjoys and does instinctively rather than being driven by pangs of hunger.

The cat is a carnivore which means that its natural diet consists of the prey which it eats. The cat's teeth and whole dietary adaptation are geared towards the consumption and digestion of entire insects, small rodents, birds, amphibians and fish. While cats do eat some plant matter, they have specific requirements for certain nutrients that can only be found in animal tissues. For this reason, meat must form at least part of a cat's diet. For an owner to try to impose a vegetarian diet would be cruel.

Nutrients are the part of the food that provide energy or raw materials from which the cat builds or replaces its tissues. Unless they are provided in the correct quantity and balance, the cat will not be able to maintain a normal, active life. Nutritional requirements vary at different stages of the cat's life cycle, which is why commercial cat foods are now available for kittens, adults and senior cats. The belief that feeding a cat well makes it less likely to bring its prey into the

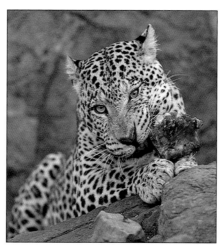

house, or that keeping the cat hungry will make it become a better mouser, is ill-founded. A cat does not need the incentive of hunger to hunt; the healthier it is, the more successful it will be as a hunter.

♦ LEFT
A leopard with its natural prey. Even a domestic cat will appreciate the occasional raw bone.

♦ BELOW
Abandoned kittens enjoy a balanced diet and security at a cat welfare home.

ROUTINE

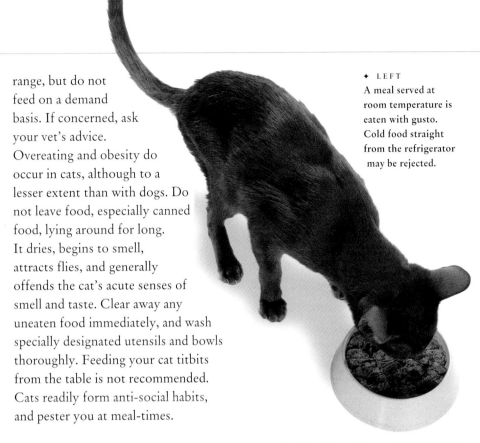

Feed an adult cat once or twice a day. Serve the food in the same place at around the same time each day. A mixture of canned and dry food is a good idea, for variety, and so that the cat uses its jaws and teeth on the dry food. For the correct quantity, follow the manufacturers' recommendations on the can or packet. An adult 4kg (8lb) cat generally needs around 400g (14oz) of canned food per day or about 50g (2oz) of dry food, depending on its lifestyle. Cats with freedom to roam will need more than an indoor cat, and more may be required during cold weather. Avoid giving snacks between meals. If your cat asks persistently for more, check the quantities are within the above range, but do not feed on a demand basis. If concerned, ask your vet's advice. Overeating and obesity do occur in cats, although to a lesser extent than with dogs. Do not leave food, especially canned food, lying around for long. It dries, begins to smell, attracts flies, and generally offends the cat's acute senses of smell and taste. Clear away any uneaten food immediately, and wash specially designated utensils and bowls thoroughly. Feeding your cat titbits from the table is not recommended. Cats readily form anti-social habits, and pester you at meal-times.

◆ LEFT
A meal served at room temperature is eaten with gusto. Cold food straight from the refrigerator may be rejected.

◆ ABOVE
A Siamese can persistently ask for more food in a very loud voice. Some indoor/outdoor cats do need more food in cold weather, or simply because they are more active than indoor cats.

◆ RIGHT
A cat takes its meal on a worktop, so that the house dog does not steal its food. Ideally, the area should not be used for human food preparation. A windowsill is more suitable.

A BALANCED DIET

Within its diet the cat requires a balance of proteins, carbohydrates, fats, vitamins, minerals and water. If you give your pet meals at regular times, and offer a variety of fresh and commercial cat foods following the guidelines below, it should get all that it needs without the addition of any dietary supplements such as vitamin pills. Read the labels of commercial cat foods to check the nutritional contents.

PROTEINS FOR STRENGTH

Proteins are made up of amino acids which are the building blocks of the body. They are not only used for growth and repair, but they can be metabolized to provide energy. The amount of protein in a cat's diet depends on its age. As cats become less active with age, they need a less protein-rich diet. In addition, their livers and kidneys have reduced efficiency and are less able to flush out the toxic by-products produced from the body's breakdown of proteins. A kitten, however, because it is growing and building up its muscle mass, needs around 50 per cent of protein in its diet, compared with over 30 per cent

◆ LEFT
Cats enjoy a varied diet and are not averse to raiding the owner's food supplies to achieve it.

◆ BELOW
Natural instinct is the driving force for a cat to hunt, not hunger. Feeding your cat a healthy and adequate diet will not stop it hunting, and could improve hunting performance.

◆ BOTTOM
A pair of Singapura kittens clearly have sufficient animal fats and tissue in their diet to provide them with an abundance of energy.

for a young adult. These levels are around 20 per cent more than those required by a dog of comparable age. The cat's digestive system processes proteins so efficiently that only 5 per cent of total protein absorbed is lost through waste products. Regular ingestion of protein must occur or the cat loses weight and condition. In the wild, feral cats acquire the essential amino acids through a variety of captured animals. Protein-rich foods are meat, fish, eggs, milk and cheese. Today, all nutritional needs are covered in the commercially available, scientifically formulated cat foods.

FATS FOR ENERGY

Fats are the second major source of energy for cats and should form a minimum of 9 per cent of the dry matter of the diet. The cat can digest up to 95 per cent of the fat it consumes; any excess is stored beneath the skin to provide insulation and protection for the internal organs. However, an imbalance between intake and fat used up through normal exercise can lead to an excess of fatty deposits and obesity. Fat is broken down in the body to fatty acids, which are important in the formation and maintenance of cell membranes throughout the body. In addition, fat also provides fat-soluble vitamins to the cat, including vitamins A, D, E and K. Some fatty acids are essential to the cat's diet, and are almost entirely absent from vegetable foods. They come from animal fat and tissue.

CARBOHYDRATES FOR BULK

Carbohydrates are the major energy source for most animals, but the cat can, in fact, survive without them. The

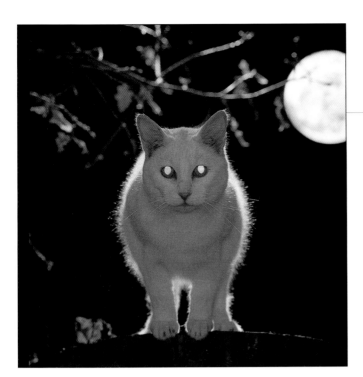

◆ LEFT
Night vision can be helped by vitamin A.
This should be provided by a balanced diet
that includes some liver, for example.

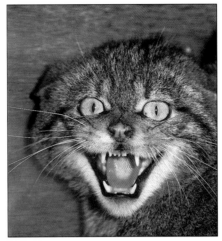

◆ LEFT
The teeth of the wild
cat and its domestic
descendants are
geared to killing and
eating small animals.
A vegetarian diet
would not be
appropriate for
your cat.

cat's main natural food sources, birds
and mice, are relatively low in
carbohydrates, apart from what is
found in the stomachs of the prey.
However, carbohydrates are a
considerably cheaper energy source
than protein-rich meat and fish, and
are therefore usually incorporated into
most commercial cat foods.

Carbohydrates can provide a
beneficial boost of readily available
energy at times of growth, pregnancy,
nursing or stress. They are also a
useful source of fibre, which although
not digested by the cat, provides
bulk in the faeces. A wild cat would
obtain fibre from the fur, feathers or
stomach contents of its prey, but the
domestic cat obtains it from most
commercial cat foods in the form of
cellulose or plant fibre.

Carbohydrates should not make up
more than 40 per cent of the diet.

MINERALS AND VITAMINS

Proteins, fats and carbohydrates
are macronutrients, whereas vitamins
and minerals are micronutrients –
they are required in only small
quantities. A cat synthesizes vitamin C
for itself, and therefore needs no

extra. Vitamins A, D, E and K work
together to refine the bodily
functions, and they should all be
present in a healthy, balanced diet,
together with the vitamins of the B
complex. An excess of vitamins can be
harmful. Cats fed exclusively on liver,

for example (which they love because
of the high fat content), may be
getting an overdose of vitamin A
which is stored in the liver. This can
lead to serious arthritic problems
involving the legs and spine, even in
young cats.

◆ ABOVE AND ABOVE RIGHT
Commercially available snacks, such as these biscuits and milk-flavoured
drops, should be given in ones and twos, as an occasional treat, not in
bowlfuls as a main meal.

◆ RIGHT
A determined
attempt to reach the
treats at the bottom
of the jar is likely to
end in success. It is
wise to keep
cat-friendly food in
sealed containers in
cat-proof cupboards
if you do not want
your pet to help
itself at will.

63

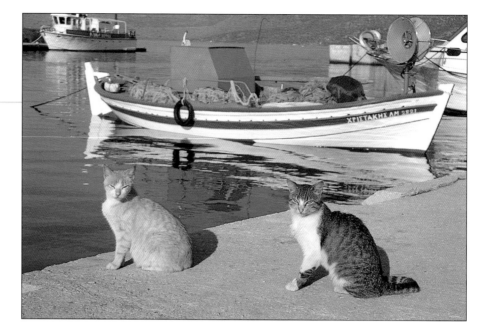

Minerals need to be available in the correct amounts which, in turn, have to be correct in relation to each other. The daily requirements even of macro minerals (which include phosphorus, calcium, sodium, potassium and magnesium) are measured in milligrams (one thousandth of a gram). Trace or micro minerals are also necessary, but daily requirements are measured in micrograms (a millionth of a gram). A cat that has a regular and balanced diet is unlikely to suffer from mineral deficiency, and supplements should not be necessary.

Calcium and phosphorus, for example, are both present in milk, and are very important for the growing kitten. Kittens fed on an all-meat diet and deprived of adequate supplies of milk will develop serious bone abnormalities because they are receiving too much phosphorus (present in meat protein), and not enough calcium. For many years, Siamese breeders weaned their kittens on to a meat and water diet in the belief that milk caused diarrhoea. As a result, bone problems often occurred.

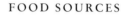

◆ ABOVE
Greek feral cats fend for themselves on the harbourside, their diet of fish supplemented by scraps thrown by tourists from the tavernas.

◆ ABOVE
A raw meat treat for a kitten exercises its jaws, cleans its teeth, and reminds it of its natural diet. It is a good idea to serve it outside!

FOOD SOURCES

You can supplement your cat's canned or dry commercial food for the sake of variety. It is obviously more time-consuming to prepare special meals, but leftovers and scraps can introduce different tastes and textures with minimal effort and preparation. It is essential, however, to have an idea of the benefits and drawbacks of certain foods, and the danger of an unbalanced diet, such as too much liver and vitamin A. If you want to feed your pet exclusively on home-prepared foods, it is advisable to discuss this with your vet, particularly with regard to types, variety and amounts.

FRESH MEAT

A house cat may traditionally have lived off table scraps and odd bits of meat and fish thrown out for it – which probably provided perfectly good nutritional levels. The feral cat will eat a small rodent in its entirety, including bones, innards and muscle and will benefit from all the nutrients these contain.

If you want to feed your cat on raw meat, this must be supplemented with other foods, such as pasta and vegetables for carbohydrates, minerals

◆ BELOW
A pedigreed cat not interested in its food could be ill or simply not hungry. It may also be bored with the same meal served up yet again and be yearning for variety.

◆ LEFT
A Red Tabby tucks into a meal served up on a plate. It is important, for reasons of hygiene, that the plate is reserved especially for him.

and fibre, that will provide the equivalent nutritional content of the bones and intestines of the naturally caught rodent.

The best meat, irrespective of type, has a valuable protein content of about 20 per cent. It is best served raw or lightly cooked as many of the vitamins can be destroyed, and the proteins denatured in the cooking process. Protein decreases and fat content increases as the cuts of meat become cheaper. Fat is not a problem, as the cat is well able to digest it and convert it into energy.

Poultry can be served, giblets and all, but make sure the bones are removed, as they become brittle with cooking and could be dangerous. Large pork or lamb bones, however, can provide a cat and kittens with hours of gnawing pleasure and also help to develop jaw strength, keep the teeth clean, and reduce the risk of dental problems in old age. Generally, avoid meats with additives and high salt content such as ham, bacon and sausages. Offal, such as liver and heart, is rich in minerals such as iron, but is also rich in vitamin A, too much of which can cause serious arthritis.

FISH
Uncooked fish has a protein level of over 10 per cent, while fish roes have a high protein level of 20–25 per cent. Raw fish should only be a rare treat, however, as it contains an enzyme that destroys some essential B vitamins. This could result in a variety of symptoms affecting the nervous and gastro-intestinal systems and skin. Oily fish, such as herring or sardines, is highly nutritious and is also higher in fat, making it a better choice than

white fish. A weekly meal of oily fish may help a cat to cope with the fur balls that collect in its stomach, as well as providing fat-soluble vitamins.

VEGETABLES
Cats on a diet of commercial cat food do not need vegetables. Sometimes they eat grass, which is considered to be a natural emetic and possibly a source of minerals and vitamins.

Vegetables are often included in commercial or home-prepared foods as a cheap source of protein and fibre.

DAIRY PRODUCTS
Milk has a useful fat and protein content, as well as lactose (milk sugar), all of which can be beneficial during periods of growth, pregnancy, lactation or stress. Cheese and milk also provide useful minerals such as calcium and phosphorus, but are not part of the cat's natural diet, and should be an occasional treat. Too much can cause diarrhoea, particularly in an older cat. Eggs mashed or scrambled are full of protein and vitamin A, but should never be fed raw as they contain an enzyme that can also destroy some essential B vitamins.

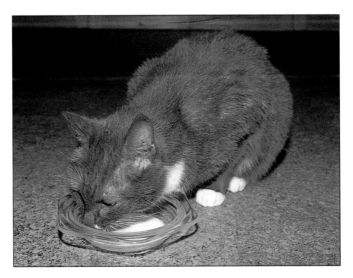

◆ ABOVE
Oily fish, such as pilchards or sardines, are nutritionally better for the cat than white fish.

◆ LEFT
Milk is a nutritious treat, but should be offered occasionally. In an older cat, it can cause diarrhoea.

65

PREPARED CAT FOOD

Over the last few decades, there has been a tremendous revolution in feline feeding methods. Today there are commercial foods available that cater for all stages of a cat's life. These are available in dry, semi-moist or canned forms, and, in addition, there are deep-frozen foods which come the closest to fresh meat or fish. If the commercial foods are manufactured by reputable, well-known brand names, you can be sure that the contents displayed on the wrapper are balanced. If they are marketed as complete foods, they are complete, and the only necessary addition is drinking water. No vitamins, minerals, or other supplements are necessary. However, cost does increase with quality, and the most expensive varieties are those that are scientifically researched and geared to the dietary needs of cats in each of the three major stages of development: kitten, active adulthood and old age.

Do check the labels for additives (preferably minimal), ingredients and breakdown of nutrient content. Bear in mind, however, that while the average protein content of a can of

◆ ABOVE
Dry food (10 per cent moisture) can be kept longer when opened and left longer in the bowl than wet food, without becoming tainted.

◆ ABOVE
Semi-moist cat food has a moisture content of 40–50 per cent, and so the cat will require less supplementary water than with a dry-food diet.

◆ ABOVE
Canned food (75–85 per cent water) dries and spoils if not eaten immediately. Supplementary biscuits provide exercise for the jaw.

food may be only 6–12 per cent, this is usually the total content per 100g (3.5oz) of food, rather than being calculated on a dry-weight basis. About 10 per cent protein in canned food is equivalent to over 40 per cent dry weight, and is therefore acceptable.

If your cat is fed an exclusively dry diet, fresh water should always be available and changed at least once a day.

WATER
Water is vital for many functions within the body. A cat can survive for 10–14 days without food, but a total lack of water can result in death within days. The daily intake depends very much upon factors such as the moisture content of the food and the climate or temperature. Cats are not great drinkers, and many will hardly seem to drink at all, as they obtain most of their needs from their food. Fresh meat and canned food are made up of about 75 per cent water, whereas dry food contains only about 10 per cent. Because of the domestic cat's evolution from desert dweller (the African wild cat), the kidneys are extremely efficient at conserving water. However, fresh water should be always available, especially if your cat eats dry or semi-moist food.

◆ LEFT
Meat is meat to these two cats; acceptable food has been found, and it will save a great deal of time and bother for their owner if they have the same thing all the time. Some cats appear to demand variety, but it is not essential for good health.

SPECIAL NEEDS

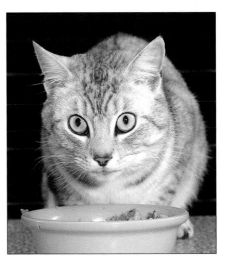

A great deal of research has gone into specialized diets for specific conditions such as heart disease, digestive disorders, lower urinary tract disease, and obesity. If you think your cat needs a special diet, seek the advice of your vet. Most of the diets are only available on prescription.

THE ELDERLY CAT

In young and adult life, cats need protein for growth, to replace worn-out tissues and also as a significant energy source. As cats grow old, they become less active, vital organs start to deteriorate, and their need for protein is reduced.

If you maintain the cat on the same diet it had when it was young and active, there will be an excess of protein. This throws strain on the kidneys and liver, as the protein has to be broken down and eliminated from the body. If the kidneys are not fully functioning due to age, the body tries to maintain the status quo by increasing thirst, and the cat starts to urinate more. This flushes out some of the toxic products, but at the same time removes some essential vitamins and minerals.

Elderly cats in general require a protein level that is reduced from 40 per cent dry weight to about 30 per cent. There needs to be a corresponding increase in fat levels to ensure that sufficient non-harmful energy is available, but not in quantities that might cause obesity. Carbohydrates (such as starches and sugars) should be avoided, as these are more difficult for the elderly cat to digest and can cause diarrhoea and other problems. Sometimes weight loss is noted in an elderly cat even though appetite has not diminished, or may even have increased. In such circumstances, consult your vet, as this may be due to a condition such as hyperthyroidism, which can be treated.

✦ ABOVE
Perhaps its owner has left stale water in the cat's bowl. In any event, the movement of the drips makes this a far more exciting way to drink.

✦ LEFT
An elderly cat's diet should supply easily assimilated protein in the right quantities to sustain energy but not overload the system.

✦ ABOVE
An active adult cat needs – and can assimilate – a higher level of protein in its diet to fuel its lifestyle than an elderly cat.

♦ LEFT
A nursing queen provides everything for her kittens, including the perfect diet, for at least the first three weeks of life.

♦ BELOW
A Brown Burmese kitten has lost its mother, but is not phased by having to join a litter of bull terrier puppies for lunch.

MOTHERHOOD

The first sign of a cat's pregnancy will probably not be a noticeable increase in abdominal size but a demand for more food. If the queen is in good condition at the time of mating, she should not need extra food until about the last third of the pregnancy (seven – nine weeks). By this time the foetuses will be growing in the womb and space is at a premium, so the cat needs frequent small meals, up to four times daily. The total quantity should only be increased by about one third. Top-quality, nourishing food of low bulk is of special importance at this time.

NURSING

To maintain the amount of milk needed for her kittens, a nursing queen will certainly at least double her normal food intake. Food should be of high quality and low bulk – in other words, as much energy and nutrients packed into as small a volume as possible. These requirements are most easily met by some of the special high-energy diets specially devised for nursing queens. Alternatively, kitten food can be used.

THE KITTENS

Kittens suckle from their mother exclusively for the first three or four weeks of their lives. As they become more aware of their surroundings they may start to nibble at their mother's food, a sure sign they are ready for

weaning. The queen will happily continue to nurse her litter to some extent well into their third month of life. However, by the time they are about eight weeks old, the greater part of the kittens' diet will usually be

provided by the owner. There is a fine line between allowing the kittens to gorge themselves, which may cause digestive problems, and giving them enough to maintain healthy growth. The weaning process should be

♦ BELOW
A Burmilla introduces her kitten to grown-up food. Good-quality kitten food will be as nourishing for a still-nursing mother as it is for the growing kitten.

The young, active adult cat often cannot last a whole day before the next meal and will need an extra snack in-between.

A Persian kitten matures over four years and frequent, nutritious meals need to be given during this time.

gradual, and the kittens fed little and often, with small quantities of high-protein food well chopped so as to be easily consumable. The easiest method of weaning is to use one of the readily available, well-established kitten foods, either in the dry or canned versions.

During the actual weaning process, canned foods are probably preferable, as the kittens may be attracted by the meaty smell. However, the dry foods are just as nutritious and have proven success. Do plan feeding times carefully so that mother and kittens may eat the extra meals in peace, away from other animals or disturbance in the household.

HOW MUCH, HOW OFTEN?

At about eight weeks old, kittens should be fed little and often. If you are feeding dry kitten food (which can be left out for longer than canned food), you can try providing it on a continuous basis for the kitten to nibble as required. Such a routine should be avoided, however, if your kitten shows a tendency to be overweight. Four or more meals a day for the kittens is normal, and can be gradually reduced to about three meals by the age of three to four months, and two meals at six months.

THE YOUNG ADULT

The feeding regime can gradually be reduced to one main meal as the kitten reaches adulthood at nine to twelve

months of age. However, young, active cats will become very hungry if they have to wait 24 hours between meals. Many owners therefore offer a snack in the morning, with the main meal at night. If this is done, it is important to ensure that the main meal is reduced in quantity by the equivalent of the earlier snack, so that too many calories do not lead to weight problems. Most breeds of cat reach their adult size at about a

year of age, although some of the longhaired breeds continue to develop until they are about four years old.

If you do have a slow-maturing cat, it is essential to ensure that adequate food of high quality is available throughout the growth period. A routine of two or three meals a day with a dry-weight protein value of over 30 per cent should continue over the growth period in order to maintain peak development.

These 12-week-old kittens are likely to be demanding three meals a day.

Grooming

Cats are fastidious animals and devote a large part of their waking hours to
grooming themselves. A little extra help from their human friends is required
by longhaired and semi-longhaired cats. Even for shorthairs, the grooming
process is important. It can be a pleasurable, bonding and rewarding experience
for both cat and owner. Extra grooming also contributes to general health, for
it stimulates the blood vessels just below the skin and improves muscle tone.

◆ FACING PAGE
A ginger cat uses his paw to clean the
parts the tongue cannot reach. The
paw stimulates secretions from the
glands on the head, which it then
transfers to other parts of the body.

◆ ABOVE
A satisfied customer – a Burmese Red –
poses for photographs after a
grooming session.

THE NATURAL WAY

The cat is well-equipped to groom itself: tongue, teeth, paws and claws are all pressed into service. The cat's tongue has a rough surface which, combined with saliva, helps to remove grit and sticky substances from the fur. Even though cats are very flexible, there are areas they cannot reach directly with the tongue – so the front paws are licked and used rather like a face flannel (washcloth). As the coat dries, the cat nibbles the fur back into place with its small incisor teeth and removes any foreign matter that the washing process failed to dislodge.

The back claws act almost like a wide-toothed comb and remove larger objects from the coat. The front paws stimulate slight oily secretions from glands around the head, and transfer them to other parts of the body during grooming. The cat is preening its coat with its own perfume, which can then be used to mark territory.

♦ ABOVE
A fluffy silver and white kitten shows her remarkable flexibility as she grooms her hind leg. Careful grooming is particularly important with long fur, to remove any matting that could lead to a skin infection.

CHANGING COATS

In the natural state, the cat sheds its coat once a year, usually in spring. However, the process is dependent on light and temperature. In warm, artificially heated and illuminated homes, indoor cats tend to shed throughout the year. It does not happen in one vast shedding of fur, but in discreet areas across the body so that hair loss is hardly noticed – except on the owner's carpets, furnishings and clothes.

When self-grooming at any time of the year, the cat dislodges loose fur, some of which is swallowed. This gradually builds up into a fur ball (hairball) which can eventually solidify into a pellet in the cat's intestine. Most cats automatically bring up a small fur ball every few days or so, but sometimes one can become stuck, causing loss of appetite and a rundown condition. In extreme cases, a vet may need to operate to remove the obstruction. The fur ball problem can strike at any time, although longhaired cats are most at risk. The occasional meal of oily fish may help ease the passage of the ingested hair.

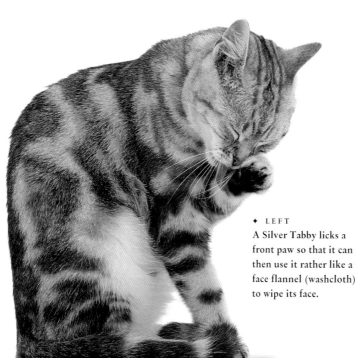

♦ LEFT
A Silver Tabby licks a front paw so that it can then use it rather like a face flannel (washcloth) to wipe its face.

♦ BELOW
The grooming process is completely absorbing for these two kittens. As well as being necessary, grooming is an activity that cats enjoy.

HUMAN AID

A feral cat in good physical condition usually keeps itself reasonably well-groomed. Domestication and selective breeding have resulted in changes to the cat's coat, such as longer hair, that sometimes require more maintenance than the cat is able to provide for itself. Assistance is then needed from the owner. Older cats, too, may lose the motivation and energy to groom themselves and welcome extra help.

You can remove some of the loose dead hairs which accumulate just by stroking a cat. The polishing action gives the coat a beautiful sheen. Some experienced owners claim that the best time to groom a cat is just after washing the dishes, for if your hands are very slightly damp, stroking is even more effective. Thin rubber gloves have a similar effect in removing loose hair.

EQUIPMENT

The grooming equipment you need depends on the type of coat your cat has. You will also gradually discover what works best for your pet. If you have a pedigreed cat, ask the breeder's advice. First-hand experience, especially from a breeder who keeps show cats, can save time and money.

Start regular grooming as a part of a kitten's routine as soon as it comes into your household. An older cat may need some encouragement to submit to the experience, but will probably soon enjoy it immensely, if you are gentle. Choose a quiet time in the cat's observed routine, make sure all you need is accessible and settle the cat on a towel on your lap. It is pointless trying to restrain a cat that just wants to play; scratches are far less likely if the cat is relaxed.

✦ CLOCKWISE FROM BELOW
Narrow/wide-toothed grooming comb, flea comb, ball-tipped brush, slicker tail brush.

✦ LEFT
A longhaired cat is lying down on a towel specially reserved for its grooming. Having a waste (trash) bin nearby is also a wise move.

✦ BELOW
Finish off a grooming session with a stroke and hear that cat purr. Stroking also removes any stray loose hairs and gives a final polish.

GROOMING A SHORTHAIRED CAT

Supplementing the self-grooming of a shorthaired cat is really only absolutely necessary if you are showing. But an extra groom, say twice weekly, does help keep loose, dead hairs under control and off the furniture. It is also a good opportunity to check for fleas, or the onset of any ear or dental problems. In addition, the activity is pleasurable for both cat and owner. The process is, of course, far simpler than for a longhaired cat. Grooming aids can include a metal

CHECKLIST

- ✦ towel
- ✦ rubber-bristled brush
- ✦ wide-toothed metal comb
- ✦ natural, soft-bristled brush
- ✦ flea comb
- ✦ chamois leather or velvet glove
- ✦ cotton wool
- ✦ ear cleaner
- ✦ eye wipes

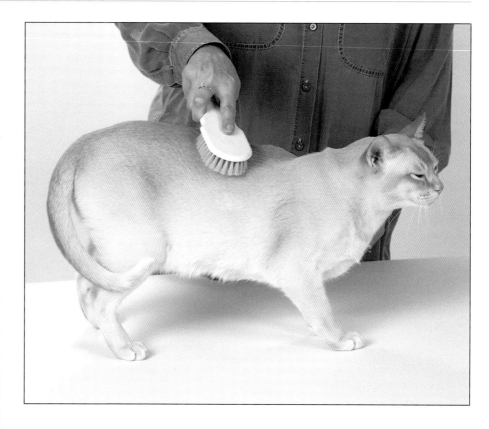

comb with round-tipped teeth, a soft, natural-bristled brush to settle the fur, a brush with stiffer bristles (a rubber brush is essential for Rex cats, as it does not scratch the skin), and a polishing cloth of silk or chamois leather. Start the grooming

session by gently stroking the cat to relax it. Use the stiff brush first, brushing very gently along the lie of the fur, to loosen the dead hairs and dirt. Brush the whole body, but be especially gentle in delicate parts around the ears, armpits and groin,

✦ **BELOW LEFT AND RIGHT**
When grooming is finished, it's time to rest and watch a friend finish off his tail. Cats often groom together if they have the opportunity; it is an important social activity.

✦ **ABOVE**
A soft-bristled brush settles the fur after any static triggered by the use of a metal comb.

and under the belly and tail. Next, use the metal comb to extract the dead hairs. It may set up some static in the coat, causing fur to clump together or the guardhairs to develop a wispy life of their own. This will be corrected with the soft-bristled brush, and a final polish with the chamois leather, velvet or silk.

A DRY SHAMPOO

It is rarely necessary to wash a shorthaired cat unless it is a pale-coloured exhibition cat, or unless the cat has become greasy – from sitting under a car, for example. Some exhibitors give their shorthairs a bran bath to remove excess grease, dirt and dandruff. Warm a good five or six handfuls of natural bran flakes in the oven to a comfortable hand-hot temperature. Rub these over the cat, avoiding the face and inner ears, working the hands thoroughly

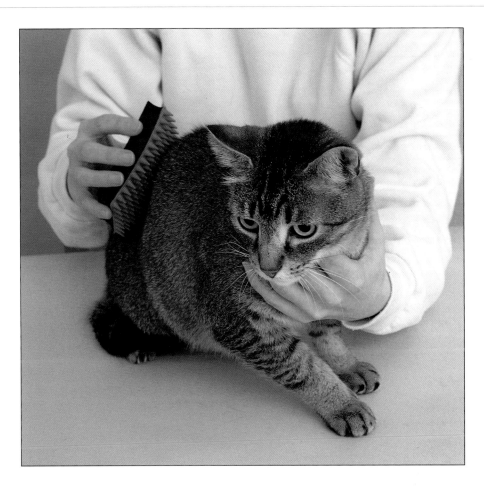

◆ LEFT
A final sheen is encouraged on a shorthair's coat by stroking it with a chamois leather or velvet glove. A silk scarf would do the job just as well.

through the coat; then simply brush it all out with a soft brush. A coat that is predominantly dark will take on a shine immediately; pastel blues and creams may take a couple of days before their texture and shine reach the peak of perfection.

◆ RIGHT
A contented and very sleek Red Burmese following a full grooming session.

GROOMING A LONGHAIRED CAT

Longhaired cats, whether they are Persians or semi-longhairs – the so-called self-grooming breeds such as the Maine Coon Cat or Norwegian Forest Cat – all need considerable grooming help from the owner. This is true whether the animal is purebred or not. Longhaired cats pick up dirt and debris in their coats, and they need help to keep the fur clean and free from tangles. This must be done daily. If not, the hair mats, particularly in the armpits and groin, and can become uncomfortable. A severely matted coat is unyielding and prevents the cat from moving with ease. Any movement results in individual hairs being pulled. The build-up of fur leads to deterioration in the general condition of the coat and a much greater likelihood of hairballs.

Grooming procedures are more elaborate than for the shorthairs. Start with the wide-toothed comb with blunt teeth to ease out tangles and debris. Try the comb on yourself before you try it out on the cat. If it does not feel sharp on your head, it should be fine for the cat. To deal with obstinate knots and tangles, sprinkle them with unscented talcum powder and ease them free with your hands. A sprinkle of talcum powder also helps pick up excess grease and dirt. It should be brushed out thoroughly at the brushing stage. Make partings in the tail, and brush each parted section sideways. Finish with a well-earned stroke in all the right directions.

1 Use the comb gently to ease out any tangles, knots and twigs. Sprinkle with talcum powder once a week. Do the underbelly and legs first.

2 Brush the body fur firmly in sections against the lie of the fur towards the cat's head. Brush thoroughly to remove talcum powder, if you have used it.

3 Use the fine comb for the neck fur. For Persians, the fur should be combed upwards to form a ruff beneath the chin.

CHECKLIST FOR SHAMPOO AND GROOM

- ✦ towels
- ✦ wide-toothed metal comb
- ✦ fine comb
- ✦ natural-bristled brush
- ✦ unscented talcum powder
- ✦ feline or baby shampoo
- ✦ shower attachment
- ✦ hairdryer

✦ RIGHT
A Maine Coon is groomed fit for going on exhibition.

SHAMPOO AND STYLE

Washing a cat is time-consuming, but essential if you are to show your cat. Unless the idea is introduced during kittenhood, a cat may object to being bathed, so it is helpful to have two pairs of human hands.

Make sure the room is warm, free of draughts, and escape-proof. A large, flat-based kitchen sink is ideal. Allow plenty of clear space around the sink, with a stock of dry towels nearby, and one on the draining board. Have all you need at hand before you start.

1 Fill the sink with warm water to about 5cm (2in). Talk soothingly to the cat all the time. Using a shower attachment, test the water first, then wet the fur thoroughly. Apply a little shampoo and work into a lather. Make sure no shampoo goes near the cat's eyes, nose or mouth.

2 Rinse thoroughly and repeat the shampooing process. If you are using conditioner, put a drop on the back and work it through the coat with the wide-toothed comb. Rinse thoroughly and then squeeze down the whole body, legs and tail to remove excess moisture.

3 Lift the cat from the sink and wrap it immediately in a towel. Rub gently to absorb most of the water. You may need several towels!

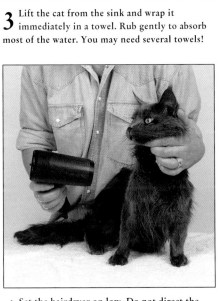

4 Set the hairdryer on low. Do not direct the airstream too close. Lift and comb the fur as you dry (this is easier if the dryer is on a stand), and stop when the fur is still slightly damp and tacky. If your cat objects to a hairdryer, do not persist, but resort to towels, brushes and patience.

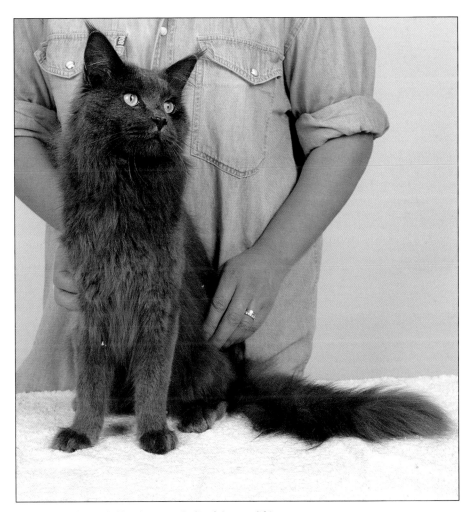

5 Use the soft-bristled brush against the lie of the coat, lifting and brushing as you go. Separate any knots gently with the fingers. Pay particular attention to the flow of the tail plume. Make sure the leg fur is well separated, and that the fur on the underparts, particularly in armpits and groin, does not become curly. On Persians, work up the dramatic ruff of fur around the neck.

ATTENTION TO DETAIL

EYES
The discharges that accumulate in the corners of the eyes can be removed carefully with your finger. Short-faced cats are prone to show tear stains beneath the eyes, which can be cleaned with a special preparation available from pet stores or the vet's surgery.

MOUTH AND NOSE
A dark brown or black tarry secretion on the cat's chin indicates an excess production of sebum from the hair follicles, which is used in scent marking. A similar condition, known as stud tail, can occur around the base of the tail. Veterinary treatment is usually necessary. Recurrence may be prevented by cleansing with special anti-bacterial shampoo from your vet.

TEETH AND GUMS
Keeping your cat's teeth clean reduces the risk of gum disease which has escalated with the advent of modern

◆ BELOW
A cat is more inclined to allow its teeth to be cleaned if the toothpaste is flavoured with chicken, fish or meat.

cat foods. If tartar can be kept under control, the risk is reduced. Some vets give cats a general check-up once or twice a year, and if necessary, perform a scale and polish under general anaesthetic. The alternative is for the owner to clean the cat's teeth once or twice a week. Special toothbrushes that fit over your finger and cat food-flavoured toothpastes make the job easier, but do not necessarily guarantee

◆ LEFT AND BELOW LEFT
Daily cleansing of the area around the eyes is particularly necessary with Persian cats. This kitten is being introduced to the idea at an early age. A cotton wool bud (swab) dampened with tepid water is used, and the area is gently wiped with absorbent tissue.

◆ ABOVE
The owner cleans tartar from the outside surfaces of the kitten's teeth. The cat's rough tongue will take care of any tartar build-up on the inside surfaces of the teeth.

◆ BELOW
A shorthair has its ears checked as part of its grooming routine. A slight build-up of wax means a gentle wipe with absorbent tissue.

success. Just before feeding time, you could try wrapping a piece of fabric sticking plaster around the index finger. Smear this with a little wet cat food, and gently try to rub against the teeth while holding the head.

EARS

If ears appear soiled on the inside, wipe them out gently with a soft absorbent tissue on your finger, dampened with olive oil, liquid paraffin or ear cleaner from the pet shop. Never clean further than you can see, and do not use cotton wool buds (swabs). An abundance of dark brown, dry waxy material may indicate mites, in which case veterinary treatment is necessary.

CLAWS

Some Siamese cats and their derivatives, such as Balinese, Oriental Shorthairs and Oriental Longhairs, are unable to retract their claws completely and are therefore ill at ease on hard, uncarpeted floors. Elderly cats of any breed may have similar problems. The nails continue to grow and, because older cats take less exercise, are not worn down. Due to stiffness, they are

not fully retracted either. Trimming the nails will help. Outdoor cats should have only their front claws clipped, so that they are not completely disarmed if they meet an enemy, and will be able to climb should escape be necessary.

If claw clipping is necessary, ask the vet to do it, for a mistake could be dangerous. On light-coloured claws, a dark blood vessel can be seen. Cutting

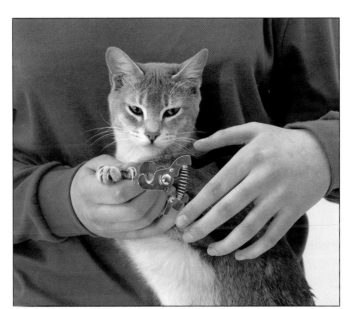

◆ RIGHT
A thorough self-groom for this cat will help keep fleas and parasites at bay, and in warm weather, help it keep cool. The saliva takes the place of sweat in humans, evaporating and cooling the cat.

this (called cutting to the quick) causes copious bleeding and pain. Declawing, or onychectomy, is considered an unnecessary mutilation in the United Kingdom. It is widely practised in the United States, and is often carried out at about the same time as sterilization. It is a major operation that removes the cat's main means of self-defence, and should be reserved for indoor cats.

◆ LEFT
A Burmese-cross is having its nails trimmed with a nail clipper custom-made for cats. Clippers designed for human nails may split cats' claws. Only the very edges are trimmed. If you are at all uncertain about your skills, it is wise to ask the vet to do this job.

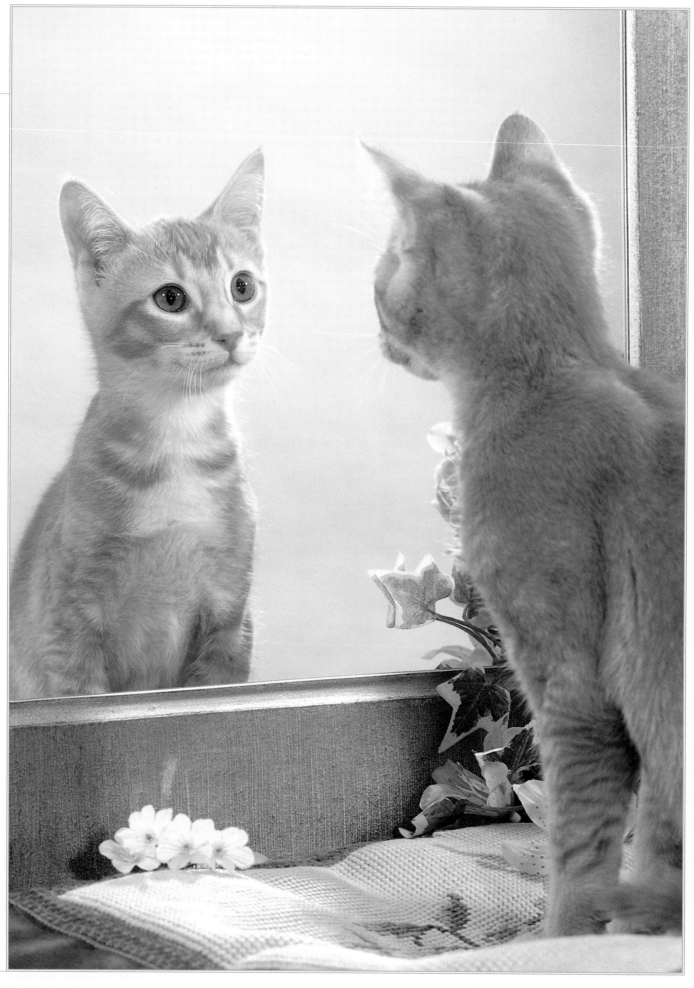

Behaviour and Intelligence

The average cat is considered to be fairly intelligent, but compared with dogs
its repertoire of party tricks appears paltry. Dogs, as pack animals, will obey
understood commands in order to seek the approval of, or a reward from, the
owner, who is considered to be the dominant pack leader. The cat is
a more solitary animal and may well understand what it is supposed to do
but choose not to comply.

◆ FACING PAGE
A kitten practises looking intelligent
in front of a mirror. Cats do not have
colour vision to the same extent as
humans, but they can recognize
mental alertness when they see it.

◆ ABOVE
The cat has the body and the build of
a hunter – and a temperament and
instinct to match.

THE ART OF COMMUNICATION

What a cat is inclined to do and what it can do are quite different. By nature and inclination, for example, cats move gracefully, daintily and sedately, yet their bodies are designed for speed and movement. When establishing a relationship with your cat, bear in mind that it will do what you ask not because it considers you dominant, but because it feels inclined to do so.

A well-balanced cat is used to being handled by its owner, and is alert, independent and inquisitive. If a cat is timid, dependent and constantly seeking attention, it may have suffered misuse or lack of socialization when it was young (6–16 weeks).

LEARNING FROM YOUR CAT

Communication is a two-way process; if you are alert and observant, you will notice subtle nuances in your cat's voice and body language. Listen to your pet in the context of its activity at the time and you may be able to link certain sounds with meanings such as hunger or contentment. Vocalization

◆ RIGHT
A well-balanced cat – confident, alert and relaxed.

and vowel sounds – miaowing – vary from cat to cat. Siamese tend to be very vocal and "talk" to their owners, other cats speak hardly at all. Purring – which can be done breathing in or out and for remarkably long, unbroken periods – is generally an indication of contentment. Kittens start to purr from approximately one week of age; they purr when they are feeding and their mother knows that all is well. It is believed that each kitten has a distinctive and unique

◆ ABOVE
A cat may be comfortably settled on its owner's lap, but its ears remain pricked and alert.

◆ LEFT
A good stretch helps keep the cat's streamlined body supple and awake, in a state of readiness for action.

purr so that the queen is able to instantly recognize which of the offspring is communicating.

Fear, anger and dissatisfaction are expressed by spits, hisses and snarls. The pitch of a growl drops when a cat is hunting to become a low hypnotic rumbling. Some cats "chitter" and salivate in anticipation or excitement when they catch sight of something to hunt. Strained, high-intensity yowls are reserved for inter-cat communication, and are especially noticeable in a female on heat.

BODY LANGUAGE

When a cat feels good, its ears are erect and forward-pointing, and its whiskers are relaxed. At rest on a familiar lap, it may purr and "knead" its paws, opening and closing them just as it did against its mother's breast when it was suckling.

If its whiskers bristle forwards, ears turn back, pupils narrow to slits, and fur, particularly along the spine and tail, stands on end, the cat is spoiling for a fight. The fur extension may be accompanied by an arched back so that the cat looks as big and menacing as possible. Wide eyes and flattened whiskers and ears are signs of fear. Whiskers are highly sensitive organs of touch and are sometimes used to make friendly contact with another cat.

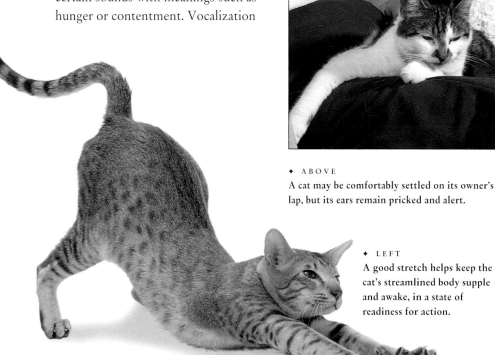

BASIC INSTINCTS

Cats are nocturnal and may spend up to 16 hours in any one day resting, if not actually asleep. As hunters, they are conserving their energy for the quick bursts of power needed to pursue their targets. Their overwhelming instinct when they go out is to hunt small creatures. This can even be detected in the play of young kittens with toys and leaves. Hearing, sight and smell are geared to the demands of stalking and hunting and these senses are much more acute than they are in humans. Tactile whiskers supplement the other senses, acting as sensors to feel close objects. They may also be used as a friendly whisker-to-whisker gesture with other cats. Cats are sociable and will establish a relationship with other animals or become part of the neighbourhood cat community if they are allowed outside. This community is hierarchical, with the unneutered (unaltered) males and females reigning supreme, and highly territorial.

GENTLE MARKING

Both male and female cats gently assert their territorial rights by rubbing their heads against objects and humans. They leave traces of a scent that is secreted by glands located at various parts of the body, but particularly around the ears, neck and at the back of the head. The scent is also released from between the paw pads when a cat scratches a tree to sharpen its claws.

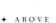

◆ ABOVE
As this cat rubs its forehead against a chair, a scent is released that proclaims the chair as part of the cat's own territory.

◆ ABOVE
At still only a couple of weeks old, this kitten has not begun to acquire trust or domesticated patterns of behaviour; it is still in its feral state, expressing fear and aggression at intruders.

◆ LEFT
A cat pounces. Its specially adapted eyes, with their wide angle of vision, are able to make the most of limited light, enabling a cat to detect the slightest movement in dim light.

TERRITORIAL RIGHTS

The cat instinctively carves out a social and hunting territory for itself. This behaviour is most marked in the unneutered (unaltered) male, whose main purpose in life is to pass on his genes to future generations. He may extend his territory to cover an area of as much as 10km (7 miles), maintaining his position in the social hierarchy and priority access to any local females by fighting. His life can be violent and short.

An unneutered female can fight as effectively and as viciously as the tom, as she develops and defends her hunting territory. From about four months of age, she periodically attracts all the males in the neighbourhood and regularly becomes pregnant.

DOMESTIC IMPLICATIONS

For the domestic neutered (altered) cat, its own home and garden are the focal points of its territory. An unneutered cat will extend the area

◆ ABOVE
A cat sprays to mark the boundaries of what it considers to be its territory. If the cat – whether male or female – has been neutered, the smell is unlikely to be obvious to humans.

◆ LEFT
Two cats demonstrate their affection for each other by rubbing their foreheads together. Other signs of friendship may include licking each other or brushing whiskers.

and challenge the neighbourhood cats. Kittens that are brought up together usually co-exist happily unless there are too many cats in the household, which could result in some territorial marking. If an adult cat is introduced into a home where there are cats already, care and sometimes expert guidance is needed. Among neutered cats, territorial rights may be resolved by some violent vocals, body language, and the establishment of non-violent dominance. If the cats are unneutered, it is a different story.

SPRAYING

The cat marks the boundaries of its patch with a spray of concentrated, very strong-smelling urine. It will also

◆ OPPOSITE
A male Burmese goes hunting: it could roam as far as 10km (7 miles) in search of food and female company if it is not neutered.

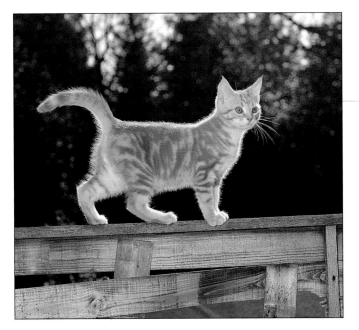

◆ RIGHT
A kitten begins to explore outside, ready to take its place among the local community and hierarchy of cats.

◆ BELOW
Son, aged six months, is keen on keeping close to his mother. The dominant, unneutered female, however, is not always this complacent, and often asserts her independence.

do this if it feels threatened or insecure, for example, if strange visitors or animals come into the house. The most common and the most pungent spraying comes from unneutered males, but entire females spray, especially when they are on heat. Neutered cats also spray, but the odour is usually less offensive.

In extreme situations, the marking may involve dropping faeces away from litter trays (pans). This is not simply dirty behaviour, but dysfunctional, and the causes must be established. A cat that constantly re-marks its territory is trying to reassure itself that it is worth something. The wise owner checks with the vet for medical advice. Home treatment of attention and affection may solve the problem. If the behaviour continues, you may be referred to an animal behaviourist.

THE EFFECT OF NEUTERING
Neutering (altering) dramatically reduces a cat's urge to exert territorial rights. Territory becomes confined to

an area around the home (although this will still be robustly defended by a neutered cat of either sex).

In a neutered, or castrated, male, the means of producing the hormones that fuel sex drive – the testes – are removed. Castration takes place ideally from four months of age. It is done under general anaesthetic. No stitches are needed, recovery is complete within 24 hours, and there is no discernible traumatic effect on the cat. Long-term, however, the animal's territorial, sexual and hunting behaviours are modified. A female is

neutered or spayed by the removal of her ovaries and uterus, or womb, so that she cannot become pregnant. She no longer comes on heat or attracts all the local males. The operation is ideally carried out from four to five months of age. Once the cat has recovered from the anaesthetic, she is usually fine. Long-term she may become more friendly and placid. Desexed animals do tend to convert their food more efficiently, and may be less active. If they start to look plump, some attention to diet may be necessary.

◆ RIGHT
Two neutered (altered) Burmese, who have known each other since kittenhood, are happy to share their limited territory of house and garden amicably.

BEHAVIOURAL PROBLEMS

◆ BELOW
The areas between a cat's eyes and ears are often more sparsely covered with fur than elsewhere. On this cat, however, the extreme baldness may be a sign of stress and be due to excess rubbing.

It is sometimes difficult to recognize symptoms of stress in the solitary, individualistic feline. Some breeds are more nervous than others. Highly strung Orientals, for example, can react very badly to strange situations, and even the first visit to a cattery may change the personality. Stolid domestic shorthairs may be equally upset, but are more likely to react aggressively – by hissing, scratching and biting. Cats probably show stress to a greater extent than dogs, but the first signs are sometimes too subtle for us to notice.

SYMPTOMS OF STRESS

When feeling vulnerable, a cat withdraws into itself, and cold aloofness is one of the first clues to its condition. A cat about to go into battle tries to appear as large as possible, but in distress it tries to become mouse-sized. Fur is flattened, tail is curled round and the cat crouches. If the situation continues, the cat starts to shake. Salivation, vomiting and defecation can also be signs of nervousness and tension.

A cat may react actively or passively when it is frightened. Typical, active signs are pupil dilation, arching back, piloerection (the hair stands on end) and hissing. A cat may react to any

attempts at reassurance, such as vocal intonations or body contact, with further aggression.

Passive symptoms of fear are more subtle and harder to detect. The cat may hide or try to appear smaller, placing the ears back and becoming immobile. A timid cat will start at the slightest movement or unexpected noise. This

may be because it was abused as a kitten, or simply because it lacked proper socialization. If you breed, it is important to socialize your kittens to prepare them for everyday household life and noise.

DEALING WITH FEAR

Mild fear may be overcome by the owner. A timid cat needs a safe, quiet place to retreat to, such as a covered bed. Avoid forcing your attentions on the cat – wait for it to approach you. Always move slowly, speak to it softly and evenly and keep strangers or strange situations at bay until it has become more confident.

It is important to identify the cause of a cat's fear so that you can deal with it. This may not always be easy, unless

◆ ABOVE
An aggressive cat seeing off an unwanted visitor. Neutering makes a cat more placid.

◆ LEFT
A timid cat crouches or hides when feeling threatened by the slightest noise or an unexpected situation.

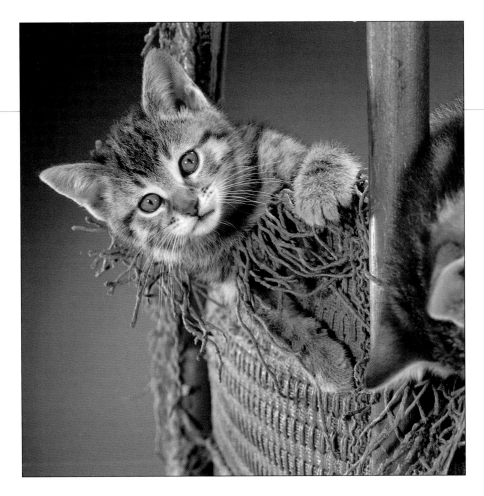

it is obvious – a one-off visit to the vet, for example. There may be an ongoing situation, such as mild teasing behaviour by a child, or persistent noise or confinement. Once the cause is established, it must be removed and the cat's confidence regained.

It may be that you can persuade the cat to overcome its fears. Cats have a highly developed flight response and when faced with any threatening situation, such as being trapped in a carrier or a car, their immediate reaction is to try to get away. You may be able to control this with soothing words or by gradually making the cat realize it needn't be afraid by exposing it little and often to the situation.

After an initial shock reaction, cats often settle down in catteries or veterinary hospitals after about 48 hours. If they are handled, however gently, during that time, they may associate the handling with the initial fear and bridle every time anyone approaches to feed them. Left alone, they usually calm down and soon start to make overtures to the very people that they hated the day before.

◆ ABOVE
Scratching is fun for the kitten, but does not do the soft furnishings much good. Provision of a scratching post and a little training should solve the problem.

DEALING WITH AGGRESSION

If a cat that is normally calm and well-behaved suddenly starts to scratch and bite, it may be ill, bored or frightened, and the underlying cause should be addressed. It is important to train a kitten from the beginning that aggressive behaviour is unacceptable, even in play. A firm no, immediate cessation of play, and a light tap on the nose whenever it bites or scratches should correct this behaviour. Do remember that a cat likes its independence, and if you impose your attentions on it when it does not want them – for example, if it is asleep – it may react instinctively by attacking you.

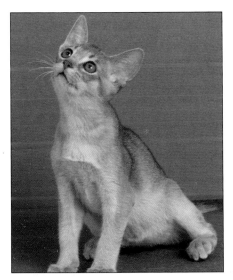

◆ ABOVE
A kitten in listening mode. It is important to talk encouragingly to your pet when it has behaved well, and never shout at it or hit it. A firm, quiet "no" and a tap on the nose should be sufficient to stop any mischief.

◆ ABOVE
Play with your indoor cat as often as you can to ensure it gets enough exercise and attention, or its boredom could turn to destructive tendencies.

TRAINING AND LEARNED BEHAVIOUR

Switched-on, intelligent cats will soon learn to manipulate doting owners. They can also be trained to produce predictable repeatable behaviour. The degree of training depends very much on the amount of time the owner has to spend with the cat. A kitten's play is, in fact, its instinctive means of acquiring hunting and survival skills.

Although many hunting actions are instinctive, they are also learned from other cats. Solitary, hand-reared kittens do not learn to hunt.

Each kitten is an individual with a unique temperament and balance of skills. In encouraging and extending a kitten's play, you can observe the strengths and weaknesses in its temperament and skills repertoire. Observing and enhancing natural

traits is the secret behind the methods of successful animal trainers. All cats show skill at balancing and spacial awareness, but some are much better than others. A kitten may pick up a piece of crumpled paper and bring it to its owner to be thrown again. You can encourage repetition of this trick with a tasty titbit and pretty soon you will be boasting about your "retriever" cat!

You can train your cat to conform to certain household standards, using spoken commands which the cat is well able to understand and respond to.

ESTABLISHING COMMUNICATION

The first step in training is to establish communication between cat and human, and a kitten should be given a name as soon as possible. If an adult cat joins the household, it is advisable to retain its existing name even if you dislike it. If you use the cat's name repeatedly when you are attracting its attention, it will soon learn to respond. From there it is easy for the cat to learn certain command words. Repetition of the verbal message, spoken firmly in a low voice, and

◆ LEFT
Each kitten is an individual with its own strengths, weaknesses and special skills. This kitten's speciality seems to be acrobatics.

◆ RIGHT
Kittens and young cats enjoy playing hide-and-seek – as long as they are found quickly, congratulated and cuddled.

◆ LEFT
The intelligent cat helps
itself to a treat.

best sofa, say no, gently but
firmly, take it to the
scratching post, and place its paws
on the post. If the cat uses the post,
give it some praise and a stroke.

◆ ABOVE
To dissuade a cat from nibbling your
houseplants, provide it with its own pot of cat
mint. You could also try wiping the leaves of
plants you want to protect with a solution of
lemon juice and water.

USING THE CAT FLAP
Practice and encouragement is also the
key to training a cat to use a cat flap.
Make sure the door is at a comfortable

never shouted, is the key. Avoid
shouting, for this can traumatize a cat
and lead to behavioural problems.

SAVING THE FURNITURE
A cat scratches a tree – or your
furniture – to sharpen its claws, to
mark its territory, or just for the
satisfying feeling. If you want to
conserve your furniture, therefore,
provide your cat with a scratching
post, and, as an extra incentive, rub
some catnip into it. Whenever the cat
begins to assault the curtains or the

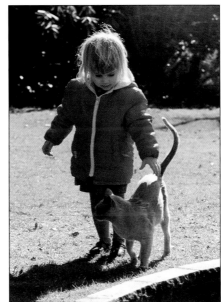

◆ LEFT
A cat enjoying the companionship of its young
owner. Although independent, most cats are
social animals and prefer to have company.

height for your cat and that the
flap swings easily. Place some
tempting food on the far side
of the door and gently push
the cat through. Then open
the flap slightly and call the cat back.
Repeat a few times and the cat will
soon learn to operate the flap itself.

◆ ABOVE
Here's a positive response to an owner's call.
From the look of expectancy and the line of the
tail, it is probably supper time.

◆ LEFT
Boy and kitten play
together. This is
important for both –
the child learns to be
gentle and kind to
animals. The kitten
does not become lonely
or bored and hones its
hunting techniques.

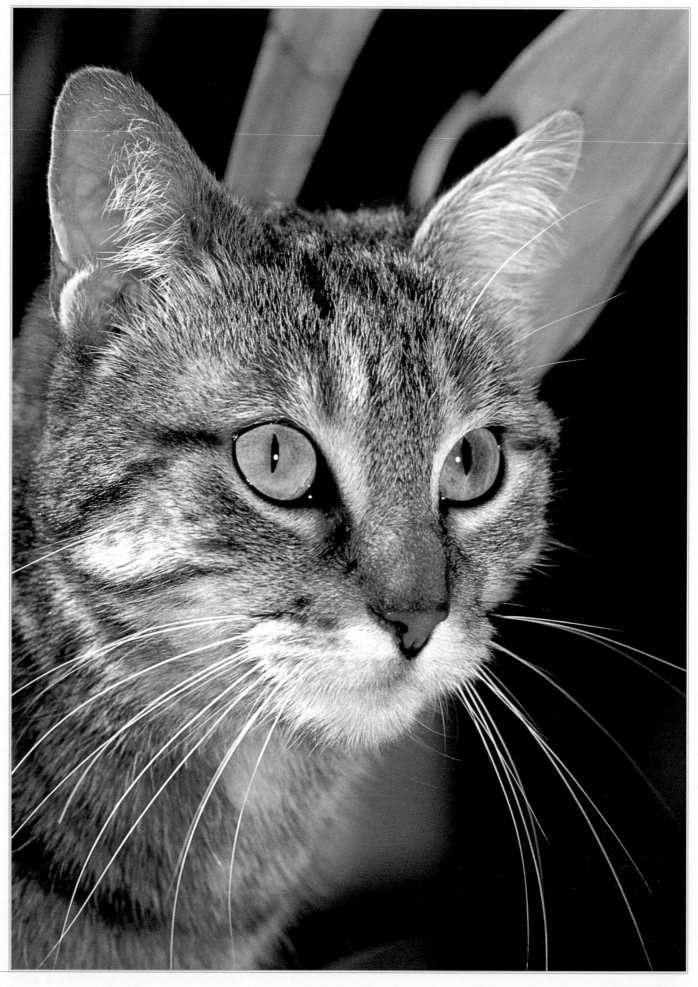

General Care and Everyday Health

A cat is a survivor, and if it is injured, will often keep going regardless, making it difficult to spot if anything is wrong. Getting to know your cat's character, giving it regular checks, and understanding a little about the strengths and weaknesses of its body will help alert you to the first signs of illness or injury. Vigilance and care will keep the vet's bills down, too. If an emergency arises, knowing how to deal with it may save your cat's life and increase its chances of a full recovery.

◆ FACING PAGE AND RIGHT
Two images of cats in prime condition. Bright eyes, alert expressions and a proudly carried tail are all indicators of sound physical and mental health.

How to Tell if your Cat is Sick

The cat's coat is a barometer of health. It reflects the quality of its diet and general condition, and should be gleaming and free from dandruff. The healthy cat's eyes are bright and clear with no discharge, redness or blinking. The tissue around them is pale pink in colour rather than red and inflamed. Nose leather is cool and slightly moist from the cat's tear ducts, and licking also keeps the nostrils moist.

Often, it is only by knowing your cat and understanding how it normally behaves, looks and reacts within its usual environment that you can tell if anything is wrong. You are the mirror of your cat's health, so do not be afraid to mention anything abnormal that you have noticed, no matter how small. The vet may only see your cat once a year and does not know its normal character or behaviour. Particular points to look out for are changes in eating or drinking habits.

SIGNS OF A SICK CAT

The first sign that your cat is not well may be a change in its normal behaviour or appearance that may only

◆ ABOVE
A Red Tabby is interested in the life going on around it, as every healthy cat should be.

◆ ABOVE
An alert expression, pricked up ears and a glossy coat suggest that this cat has a balanced diet and a healthy, contented life.

◆ LEFT
A cat playing is in character – if it were suddenly to become uninterested in playing and listless, this would be a sign to the owner of possible ill health.

WHEN TO CALL THE VET

If your cat is displaying any of the following symptoms, call the vet immediately:

◆ blood in vomit, urine or faeces

◆ excessive thirst

◆ swollen and tender abdomen

◆ high temperature

◆ vomiting and diarrhoea together

◆ bleeding from penis or vulva

◆ straining when it tries to pass urine

◆ shallow, laboured breathing

◆ after a road accident

be perceptible to you. If a normally friendly cat shows signs of aggression, or an outgoing animal suddenly becomes withdrawn, timid and shy, look for other signs of illness. Lack of response to being called may be due to fever or temporary deafness caused by ear mite infestation.

COAT
A stary, ungroomed look to the coat with abnormally raised fur is a general indication of ill health.

STOOLS
If you still have cause for concern, check the cat's stools: they should be firm and without extreme or pungent odour. If you have an outdoor cat, confine it if possible and provide a litter tray (pan), so that you can make this check.

Where cats have access to dustbins, diarrhoea may be caused by a stomach upset resulting from eating contaminated food, but could be a sign

UNDERSTANDING YOUR CAT'S ANATOMY

The cat's skeleton provides support and protection for the vulnerable, internal organs. The entire feline skeleton is strong but light, as befits its function as a hunter.

The coat normally comprises a dense, soft undercoat covered by coarser hairs which are known as guardhairs. The density of the fur adds further protection to the skin (epidermis) from which it grows.

Skin consists of many layers of cells. These are constantly reproducing to compensate for the loss caused by sloughing of the cells which die and are shed from the surface as scurf.

TAIL Tail bones are joined by a complex machinery of small muscles and tendons, making the tail capable of a great range of movement. This enhances balancing potential and has also developed as a barometer of the cat's emotional state.

EYES Deep, large eye sockets facing forward protect the eyes. Binocular vision gives the depth of focus needed by a hunting animal in order to judge distances accurately.

HEAD is that of a typical predator, with a strong skull protecting the brain. It is capable of a wide range of movement due to the very flexible neck.

EARS Large, cup-like outer ears collect a vast range of sound. This is helped by tiny muscles which give the ears great flexibility of movement. The inner ear assists with balance.

BACK The back muscles are well developed to allow the cat to carry heavy weights over long distances. The spinal column ranges from the closely positioned bones of the chest to the longer, heavier lumbar vertebrae which support the weight of the body organs.

PELVIS is fused to the vertebrae of the lower back, and these are also linked to the progressively smaller bones of the tail.

TEETH are those of a typical predatory carnivore – canine teeth, or fangs, for killing; incisors for gripping; heavy, sharp molars for chewing and tearing. This process is helped by a very flexible lower jaw arrangement which allows sideways movement so that the tearing process becomes very efficient.

FRONT LEGS are capable of some rotation so that the pads can be presented to the face, for use in the washing process.

PAWS are long so that the cat actually walks on its fingers and toes which are supported by the sensitive fleshy pads. Claws are capable of being retracted.

BACK LEGS Movement is restricted to backwards and forwards only. The way in which the knee opposes the position of the elbow at the front, allows for the enormous spring which gives the cat the ability to pounce.

of something more serious, especially if it is persistent. Constipation, causing the cat to strain, can also be a problem, especially if there is any blood in the stools.

EYES

If the third eyelid – the haw or nictitating (blinking) membrane – is visible, it indicates an infection or that there is a foreign body in the eye. Any signs of redness or inflammation or excessive and persistent, thick, yellowish discharge are cause for concern. If either pupil appears dilated or does not react to bright light, this needs prompt veterinary attention.

EARS

Clear wax in the ears is normal, but a dark brown waxy deposit may indicate ear mites that need veterinary treatment. Look out for seeds, such as grass seeds, too. A seed may lodge in the ear and enter the ear canal, making the cat shake and scratch its ear. The wall of the ear canal and flap (pinna) is

extremely delicate and vulnerable to damage in fighting situations. A puncture to the pinna often results in a haematoma (a large blood blister) that could become infected if not

treated. If the ears are very hot, the cat may be running a temperature, but before rushing to the vet, check this is not due to your cat lying in the sun or next to a radiator!

✦ ABOVE
An owner gently holds back the ear to check that there are no scratches on the pinna (the inner lining of the outer ear). Also check for dark, waxy deposits.

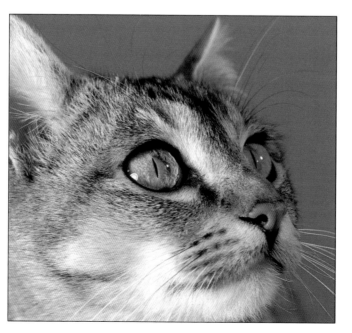

✦ ABOVE
As part of the regular care routine, make a random check in the fur by parting it until you can see the skin.

✦ LEFT
As in humans and other animals, the state of a cat's eyes can indicate problems elsewhere in the body. This cat's eyes are those of a radiantly healthy animal.

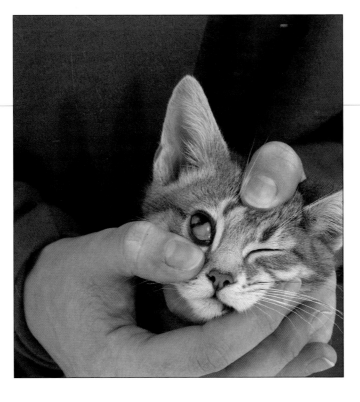

◆ RIGHT
It is important to check the cat's third eyelid, or nictitating membrane. If this shows on its own, it suggests there is something wrong. The cat may have an infection or a foreign body in its eye.

SICKNESS

Light vomiting is very often no cause for alarm. It may be due to the cat having bolted down its food too fast, a reaction to something it has caught and eaten, to grass that it has chewed to clear its system out, or a physiological response to remove hairballs. Persistent vomiting, however, especially if it contains any blood, is important, and is reason enough to check with the vet.

TEMPERATURE

A good indication that the cat has a raised temperature is if the ears feel hot. A rectal thermometer is needed in order to take a precise temperature reading, which should be 38–38.5°C (100.5–101.5°F). Unless you have been taught how to do this properly, it is best left to a professional.

PULSE

Key pulse points in a cat are located under the forearms (armpits) and back legs (groin). The pulse rate may vary between 120 and 170, depending on how active the cat has been recently. The average is 150.

REGULAR CHECK-UPS

The caring and wise owner checks the pet regularly to make sure it is in top condition. Early signs of conditions such as mite infestation or fleas will prevent more serious problems developing later. The check-up can be at a time when you are relaxing with your cat, or if it is one that needs regular grooming, as an integral part of the grooming routine. If a cat does show any signs of ill-health or

◆ ABOVE
Modern cat food does not give a cat's teeth the exercise and cleaning power that would come from hunted food. It is therefore important to check them regularly.

discomfort, you can go through the checking points described on the previous pages. Then, if you do need to take it to the vet, you can give a detailed report on anything unusual you have noticed.

FUR AND BODY

One good reason for grooming your cat regularly, even if it is a shorthair, is that you will be quickly alerted to any lumps, or signs of attack by fleas, ticks, mites or lice. If the grooming process rakes out some grit-like dirt, check further. Comb the cat over moistened absorbent paper. If the grit leaves a red stain, these are the blood-gorged faeces of fleas. If not, the cat has just been rolling in the garden.

Small, raised grey or whitish lumps indicate ticks. These can irritate the cat considerably as the tick's head is buried deep into the skin, leaving only the body visible. They should be removed as soon as possible but great care has to be taken to ensure that the head is removed as, if left behind, an abscess or sore can develop.

EARS, NOSE AND MOUTH

Check that ears are clean and free of dark waxy deposits and seeds. Even minor scratches need to be kept clean to prevent infection. Check for broken or discoloured teeth, swollen gums and bad breath, and make sure there are no lumps (enlarged glands) around the neck.

PAWS

The claws of an indoor cat need to be checked regularly in case they need clipping and to prevent them from ingrowing. Also check for any soreness or wounds on the pads.

◆ BELOW
If your veterinary practice operates an open-surgery system in which you simply turn up without making an appointment, there may be several other customers there before you.

CHOOSING A VET

Do not wait until an emergency arises before you look for a vet. It is wise to have made arrangements before you bring a new animal home. If you found the kitten locally, ask the sanctuary, home or breeder. You may be able to continue with the vet a kitten has already visited for its initial check-ups and inoculations. If the kitten is from a different area, ask friends in the neighbourhood who already own cats, or a local cat club for recommendations (addresses and telephone numbers are available from the Governing Council of the Cat Fancy in the United Kingdom, the Cat Fanciers' Association in the United States and equivalent organizations in most other countries).

WHICH VET?

Selecting the right vet for your pet is just as important as finding the right doctor for your family – but there is one great difference. While doctors only deal with one species – the human one – vets have to cope with a

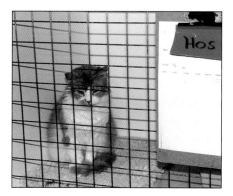

wide range of different animals, from hamsters to cows. They are unlikely to be specialized in all fields, and not all will be up-to-date with feline ailments. This may be a problem if you live in a rural area, as veterinary practices may be geared to large animals such as cattle and horses. In urban areas, most surgeries are small-animal practices, devoted to the care of cats, dogs and other small domestic pets.

If you have time contact a number of different practices; telephone first if you wish to visit. Ask for a list of fees for consultation, and the cost of routine care items such as inoculations, blood tests, flea and worming products.

QUESTIONS TO ASK

Before you go, consider what you want from the vet. If you have a neutered (altered) cat that rarely goes out, you will probably have to visit the vet only once a year for the booster inoculations, so enquire about policy for routine check-ups. If your plan is to show or breed from your cat, you

◆ ABOVE
If your pet is to have an anaesthetic, the vet may advise taking it in the night before. In this way, the surgery can control food intake and the cat has time to settle down.

◆ LEFT
A cat has its annual check. This is an opportunity for comments on general condition, any necessary booster inoculations and restocking of worming and flea treatments.

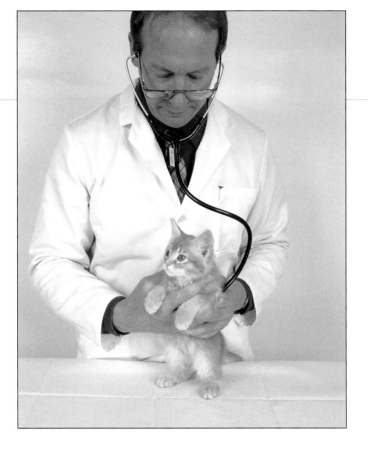

A kitten has its first check at about nine weeks. This will coincide with the first inoculations, and with pedigreed animals, will probably take place before they leave the home where they were bred.

will need to think more seriously about locating a vet who is perhaps interested in breeding, and knowledgeable about pedigreed breeds and showing. This is usually easier in a city than in a rural region.

Once you have found a practice that is cat friendly, it is worth going through a mental checklist of what you need to know.

Check opening hours. Is an appointment needed, or does the practice run on an open-surgery basis whereby you turn up unannounced between specified hours? Both can operate well in an efficient practice, but if you are working, you may need a combination of both options for maximum flexibility. You will also need to make sure that there are weekend and occasional evening surgeries.

Check that there are arrangements for emergencies around the clock. If so, will your cat be treated by one of the practice vets or a separate emergency staff? This may be significant if you have a pedigreed

◆ ABOVE RIGHT
A cat eats grass as a natural emetic – it may help to clear the system of obstructions, such as fur balls (hairballs), and provide extra vitamins.

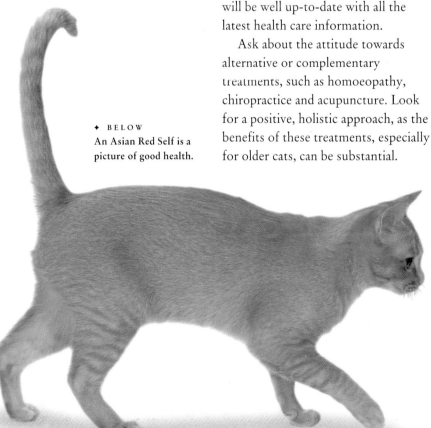

◆ BELOW
An Asian Red Self is a picture of good health.

animal that requires special attention. Also, what is the policy regarding home visits? This may be important if you are intending to breed from your cat, in case you need help at the birth. Is the practice a veterinary hospital or does it specialize in feline medicine and surgery?

If it is a member of a national advisory organization (such as the Feline Advisory Bureau in Britain) it will be well up-to-date with all the latest health care information.

Ask about the attitude towards alternative or complementary treatments, such as homoeopathy, chiropractice and acupuncture. Look for a positive, holistic approach, as the benefits of these treatments, especially for older cats, can be substantial.

STANDARD TREATMENTS

◆ BELOW LEFT
A two-week-old kitten is still gaining some immunity from infection through its mother's milk – as long as the mother herself has been kept fully up-to-date with her inoculations.

However hardy your cat is, it runs the risk of being struck down by a killer virus infection unless it is inoculated and boosted on a regular basis. If a cat contracts one of the diseases for which preventative vaccines are available, it is very serious, for there is no treatment that can be guaranteed to save it. All a vet can do is to treat the symptoms and minimize suffering, and hope that your pet's natural immunity will fight the illness.

INOCULATIONS

In the first few days of its life, a kitten's resistance is boosted by the antibody-rich colostrum that is the mother's first milk. Although this is replaced by normal milk after the first few days, this also contains some antibodies so, as long as the kittens are feeding, the mother's immunity will pass down to them through the milk. As soon as weaning starts, this natural protection diminishes. From now on, immunity has to be built up actively by the kitten and will no longer be acquired passively from the queen. Active immunity can be built up by exposure to infections or, more safely and securely, by inoculations. Taking your cat to the vet to be inoculated is a vital part of routine care. Inoculations are given at 9–12 weeks; the kitten is then kept in for a week or two to prevent exposure to infection while the aquired immunity from the vaccine becomes effective. Inoculations subsequently need to be boosted every year. Some kittens or adult cats may feel a little under par for a few days after first inoculations or the annual booster, but it is rare for there to be any major problems.

FREEDOM FROM WORRY

Over the past 30 years, there have been enormous steps forward in the prevention and cure of feline ailments. The diseases that used to pose the greatest risk to pedigreed and non-pedigreed felines alike, are no longer a problem if the regular, recommended inoculation programme is followed.

◆ LEFT
Six-week-old kittens may be introduced to new social experiences, but three weeks before their first vaccination, they must not be exposed to other cats in the outside world.

◆ BELOW
A stray cat with its single-kitten litter. The mother's tough and probably deprived lifestyle may have limited her ability to produce a bigger litter.

◆ BELOW
A kitten receives its first vaccination at six to nine weeks of age. It will have to be kept indoors for another two to three weeks after it has received its second vaccination.

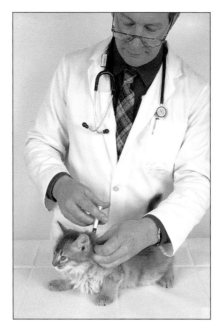

WHICH INOCULATIONS?

Recommendations regarding vaccinations vary in different countries. In the United States, for instance, where, in urban areas, owners are often advised to keep their cats indoors, both cat flu viruses, feline infectious enteritis (feline distemper) and rabies are considered the core inoculations. Those against chlamydia,

WHAT TO DO WHEN

◆ 9 weeks: first vaccination

◆ 12 weeks: second vaccination

◆ 16 weeks: spaying for females

◆ 4–6 months: neutering (altering) for males

◆ 6 months: start flea treatment

◆ monthly (after 6 months): renew flea treatment

◆ every 6 months: worm treatment

◆ every year: booster vaccinations and check-up

feline leukaemia virus and feline infectious peritonitis are often considered necessary only for cats likely to be exposed to risk in the outside world. However, bear in mind that your cat could escape and come into contact with one of the diseases you decided not to inoculate against. Take your vet's advice.

THE KILLERS

The most serious infections are: cat flu (viral rhinitis), which encompasses two viruses that affect the cat's upper respiratory tract; feline infectious enteritis; chlamydia; and feline leukaemia virus. Rabies should be added to the list in countries where the disease is known to exist. Although these are not the only viruses to affect the cat, these are the major viral conditions that have wrought havoc in the past among domestic cats.

Effective vaccines against cat flu and feline enteritis have been around for several years. A vaccine to treat the leukaemia virus is a more recent

addition. As yet, in the United Kingdom, where rabies does not exist, the vaccine can only be administered by authorised vets to cats that are going to countries where the disease exists.

GENERAL CHECK-UP

The vet will only inoculate your cat if it is in good health, so do not take it if it is below par for any reason. At the same time as the annual booster vaccinations, ask the vet to give your cat a check-up – to look at ears, teeth, gums and general condition. With luck, this will be the only time the vet sees your cat. You can also stock up with treatments for worms and fleas.

◆ BELOW
A Chocolate Silver Ocicat kitten at 15 weeks old has had all its vaccinations, and is independent of its mother.

NEUTERING (ALTERING)

Neutering, altering or desexing not only prevents reproduction but also the inconvenience of the female cat coming into heat (oestrus) or calling. In the female cat this is called spaying. In the male the operation, castration, reduces the tendency to spray and also the odour of the male cat's urine.

The operation has the effect of modifying behaviour associated with sexual desire and establishing and marking territory (see the chapter on *Behaviour and Intelligence*). The result is that the desexed cat is usually more stable and affectionate, and bonds more easily with the family. Recent work in Britain and the United States has shown that the operation in either sex can be carried out earlier than was

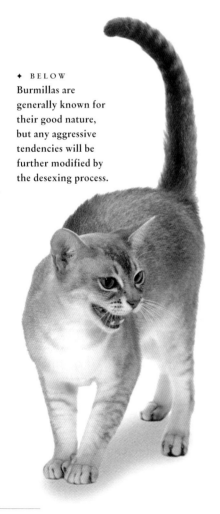

◆ BELOW
Burmillas are generally known for their good nature, but any aggressive tendencies will be further modified by the desexing process.

previously thought with no ill effects. Some rescue organizations now desex kittens before they are homed at eight to twelve weeks, but the majority of vets prefer to carry out the operation when the kitten is older, at four to six months. As both operations are carried out under a general anaesthetic, no food or water can be taken for about 12 hours beforehand. The operation cannot be reversed in either sex.

CASTRATION

The operation involves the removal, under general anaesthetic, of the cat's testes. Tiny incisions are involved and usually no stitches are necessary. Within 24 hours the cat is usually back to normal. Both kittens and adult cats can be castrated. If you consider giving a home to a stray tom, castration will ensure that he settles quickly, is less aggressive, less territorial and less

likely to roam. This also means that he is less likely to pick up infections and be involved in traffic accidents.

SPAYING

Female cats do not miss motherhood, and gain security, as they no longer have the urge to roam when coming into heat or calling, and are no longer targeted by unneutered (unaltered) male cats. Spaying or altering the female cat is more complicated than in the male. The cat's ovaries (where the eggs are produced) and womb (uterus) are removed to prevent her coming into heat. She should not be on heat at the time of the operation. A small area of fur is shaved on the abdomen and an incision made, which has to be stitched afterwards. The spayed female cat is usually back to normal quickly but will appreciate care, warmth and light meals for about a week, until the stitches are taken out.

HOW LONG WILL YOUR CAT LIVE?

◆ BELOW
A Blue Bi-colour Persian father seems to contemplate the continuation of his pedigreed line with one of his kittens.

From about the age of ten to twelve years, a cat may begin to show signs of growing old. This may not be immediately apparent as the slowing down process is very gradual. Internal organs may not work as well as they once did and joints may become that little bit stiffer. Over time the cat seems to restrict its activities, is far less playful and becomes a creature of sedentary habits. Particular health conditions such as diabetes or arthritis require constant supervision and medical intervention.

The oldest cat recorded was a tabby called Puss who was said to have lived for 36 years. The oldest pedigreed cat on record is Sukoo, a Siamese who died in 1989, at the age of 31 years. These are exceptional ages, however. Most cats live for about 14–16 years and a few may reach 20 years. With pedigreed cats there is a very accurate means of determining age, as they are normally registered with an exact date of birth and registration number.

When you first get a 12-week-old kitten, it is very likely that its lifespan will be something between ten and fifteen years. This could mean that the cat will become a companion to your children as well as to yourself. A longer life is not unusual, in which case it may well live to see your grandchildren as well. To borrow from the dog world, a cat is for life, not just for Christmas. This has to be thoroughly understood before a kitten joins the household.

Neutered (altered) cats have a slightly longer lifespan than those which remain unneutered. This is particularly true of male cats. An unneutered (unaltered) tom will fight

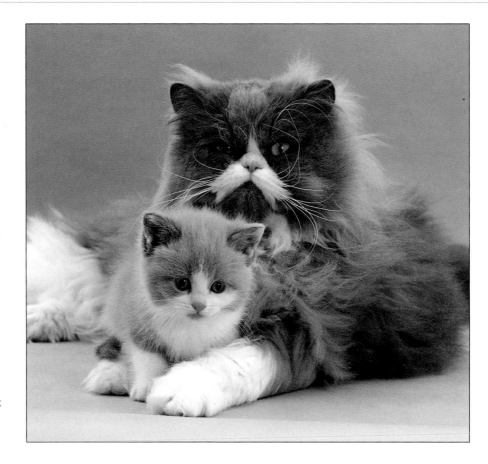

to defend territory and the resulting injuries and infections may shorten his life. Females lead a much quieter life, and a career spent having kittens, in an environment in which her condition is well-maintained, appears to have little effect on the female's longevity.

Apart from differing nutritional requirements at various stages of its life, a cat's physical responses slow down as it gets older and joints become stiff. This not only has the effect of reducing suppleness and agility, but has implications for the daily care of the cat such as grooming.

◆ RIGHT
The start of a long relationship: this kitten will probably live long enough to be a companion for its young owner throughout her childhood and teenage years.

COPING WITH DEATH

When the end comes, it can be rapid, as though a clockwork motor has run down. Very old cats settle into a routine which reflects their capabilities. It seems important for a cat to maintain its dignity to a degree greater, even, than that of many other animals. This can be extremely difficult when the efficacy of bodily functions is being challenged by old age. A few elderly cats are distressed by the loss of vital sensory equipment through deafness or blindness. Grooming becomes difficult as flexibility is reduced, and incontinence may occur, both of which can upset the naturally fastidious cat.

Your cat may die in its sleep but this does not happen often. If, however, it is suffering from ailments that give it chronic pain or prevent it from responding to its natural instincts, you need seriously to consider how kind it is to keep it alive. A vet can end an animal's life painlessly on the request of its owner. The cat is injected with an overdose of anaesthetic which literally puts it to sleep. Many vets will allow you to be present for your pet's last moments, if you wish. Others can only advise; the

✦ ABOVE
A rather portly middle-aged cat that will have to lose some weight if it is to have a healthy and trouble-free old age.

✦ BELOW
Producing two to three litters a year has left this 10-year-old farm cat with a sagging stomach. It would be kind to have her spayed.

✦ ABOVE
A 10-year-old tabby and white that could well have several more years of contented living as long as a healthy diet is maintained and disease and infection do not strike.

owner must make the decision, except in exceptional circumstances when the vet takes responsibility. Euthanasia can be regarded as a final gift to an animal that has shared your life.

MOURNING

The natural lifespan of a cat is a fraction of human life expectancy, and yet a cat may be a day-to-day companion over a significant section of your life, such as your entire childhood. When your cat dies, you may consider burying it in the garden, in a favoured snoozing spot, for instance. If not, there are pet cemeteries where cremation or burial can be carried out.

There will inevitably be a period of mourning which may, initially at least, feel as intense as it would for a member of your human family. This is quite normal. You have lost a member of the family and a very special one. This is

✦ RIGHT
Two old friends have aged in different ways. Perhaps the overweight male on the chair should give up his seat for the thin and frail female.

the little furry body that snuggled up to you when you were feeling ill, depressed or annoyed. You will remember the rumbling purr of greeting and trust, and the times when you could not express your feelings to anyone else but the little cat that listened and soothed you into eventually finding a solution.

✦ LEFT
An 8-week-old Cream Burmese kitten with a lifetime ahead of it, lives for the moment with its toys.

✦ ABOVE RIGHT
A cat grows old with dignity and favours warm spots such as the top of the stove, but beware of the danger a hot stove may present.

✦ RIGHT
A gravestone and rose commemorate the passing of a much-loved cat.

Injuries and Ailments

Cats traditionally live longer than dogs. Twenty years is not unusual. If you provide a balanced diet, the correct inoculations and regular check-ups, there is no reason why your cat should not live a long and happy life. However, illness or injury can strike at any time, so it is important to keep an eye open for any unusual behaviour in your pet that might indicate all is not well. In most cases of injury or disease, you will need to call the vet, but much can also be done at home in the way of first aid and general nursing.

◆ FACING PAGE
An injured leg is a stressful situation for a while, but the adaptable cat will adjust until the injury has healed.

◆ ABOVE
Although this cat had to have one of its legs amputated, it is able to lead a full and active life.

HOME NURSING

A sick cat should be confined in an area that is warm and free from draughts, quiet and capable of being easily cleaned and disinfected. The first two requirements are relatively easy to fulfil, whereas the third could cause some problems. Many modern homes are carpeted throughout which makes disinfecting difficult. If there is not a separate utility room with a floor that is easily cleaned, you should consider buying a large, plastic travelling carrier which comes apart so that every part can be thoroughly cleaned.

Use a disinfectant agent recommended by your vet – it is most important to avoid any substances containing coal-tar, wood-tar, phenol, cresol and chloroxylenols. These

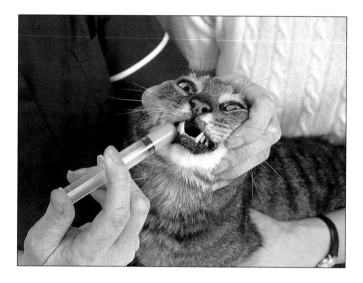

◆ LEFT
Special syringes, available from your veterinary practice and some pet shops, will help you administer medicines.

◆ BELOW
A warm, comfortable bed and plenty of tender loving care are essential.when nursing a sick cat.

agents are fine for use with people but can be lethal for cats. If a condition is seriously infectious to other cats, you should set aside some old clothes and shoes to wear when handling the sick

cat, and wash thoroughly afterwards. Always dispose of any used bandages or applicators promptly. Thoroughly clean up any vomit or faeces without delay and disinfect the area carefully.

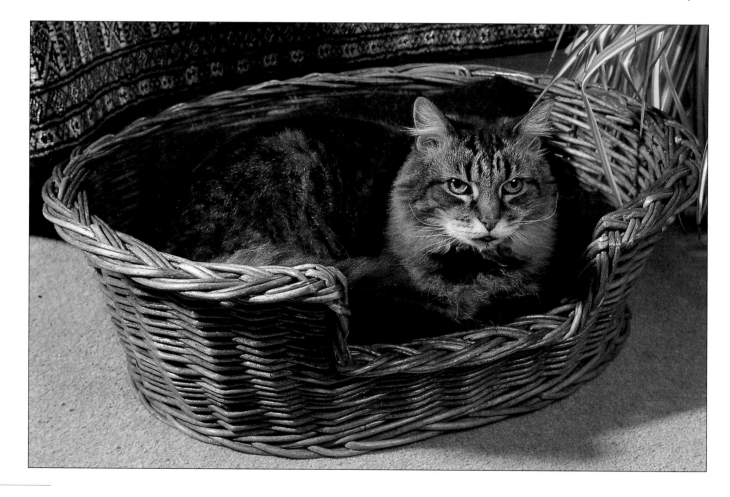

BEDSIDE MANNER

You can help your cat's recovery tremendously with care, love and attention. Spend time talking quietly, maintaining appropriate physical contact without being overwhelming, and ensuring that its bodily needs are catered for. The cat may not be able to do anything for itself and, therefore, feeding, watering, grooming and assisting with toilet procedures become your responsibility. While this is very time-consuming, the bond you have already achieved with your cat will grow even stronger. The veterinary nurses (technicians) will help if you need advice on the various techniques involved with the grooming, feeding and toileting of a sick cat.

ADMINISTERING MEDICINES

Your vet will always give advice and instruction on how much and how often you should administer any medication your cat needs for treatment. Medicinal preparations come in several forms – liquids, pills, capsules, drops and lotions. The secret of administering any of these successfully and with least disturbance to the animal is to have confidence in your ability to do so. However, some cats will object tooth and claw to having any foreign object forced into their mouths. If this is the case with your cat, you will need to ask someone to assist you and, if necessary, wrap the cat securely in a towel to help immobilize it.

Liquid medicines can be given using a plastic syringe obtainable from your vet or from most pet shops. After use it should be cleaned thoroughly and then stored for future use in a sterilizing agent such as one of those used for baby feeding equipment. Draw up the amount for one dose into the syringe. Holding the cat's head firmly, gently insert the syringe between the lips, at the side of the mouth. Push the plunger gently so that the cat receives the dose slowly and gradually, allowing it time to swallow. This reduces the risk of any liquid going into the lungs, which could cause pneumonia to set in rapidly in the case of a sick cat. Pill poppers which look like elongated syringes are available if you have difficulty opening your cat's mouth. The pill is placed into the popper and a plunger pushes the pill to the back of the cat's tongue. Direct the instrument towards the palate rather than pressing on the tongue. Hold the cat's mouth closed and stroke its throat until it has swallowed.

DROPPING IN

Most preparations designed to be dropped into the eyes or ears are supplied with a dropper or a dropping nozzle. If not, droppers can be purchased from chemists (drugstores). Always carefully read the directions about how and when to apply the medication, before using.

The membranes of the eyes and ears are very delicate and it is most important for the cat to be held securely. Another pair of hands makes the job much easier.

With eye drops, one drop is usually sufficient. For ear drops, hold the pinna (ear flap) firmly to open the canal, and place two or three drops into the ear, then massage gently. Ear drops are usually oily and overdoing the drops results in a greasy head.

ADMINISTERING TABLETS

1 Hold the cat's head firmly, with your fingers on either side of the jaw, and gently pull the head back until the jaws open.

2 Talking quietly and encouragingly to your cat throughout the process, drop the pill or capsule at the back of the cat's tongue.

3 Hold the mouth closed and massage the throat until a swallowing action shows that the pill or capsule has been ingested.

ACCIDENT AND INJURY

Emergency treatment is often required for accidents within the home. Do not assume that a cat or kitten will automatically know its physical limits or be able to tell, for example, which plants are poisonous. It might well be able to fall from any angle and regain its footing, but only within certain heights. A cat falling from a balcony is just as likely to sustain serious damage as any other animal. Cats can be as vulnerable to accidents as children, and you should keep a constant eye on safety in your home.

It is valuable to know what on-the-spot treatment you can give before the cat receives veterinary attention. In extreme situations, this could make the difference between life and death. A cat that is very frightened or in pain may instinctively withdraw, and scratch and bite if handled. If this

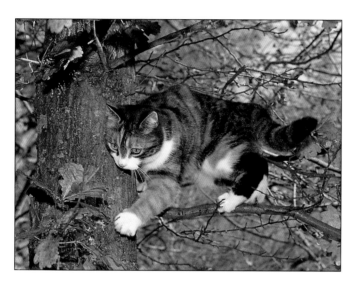

✦ LEFT
A cat is so intent on stalking a moving leaf or insect that it may end up on a branch that cannot support its weight and fall.

happens, talk calmly and keep the cat as warm, comfortable and confined as possible until professional help is available. As with any emergency, the first rule is not to panic and the second is to rely on your common sense. However inexperienced, you will learn by careful observation to recognize the real emergency. Prompt first aid is all that is needed, but if you are in the least doubt about the seriousness of any condition, seek professional help immediately. All veterinary practices have to offer a 24-hour emergency service. Phone the surgery number first to check for any special emergency arrangements, or at least to give the surgery advance warning of your imminent arrival.

A cardboard box is a good carrier in an emergency; if an injured cat is placed on a board serving as a stretcher, it could easily fall off. Keep the cat warm by covering with a blanket and call the vet immediately. Try not to panic and handle the cat as gently as possible.

THE FIRST-AID KIT

✦ sterile pads and dressings	✦ ear cleaner
✦ bandages: 2.5cm and 5cm (1in and 2in) widths	✦ liquid paraffin
✦ stretch fabric adhesive strapping	✦ kaolin mixture
✦ lint padding or cotton wool roll	✦ antihistamine cream
✦ cotton wool balls (uncoloured)	✦ rectal thermometer
✦ antiseptic wipes, cream and lotion (as recommended by your vet)	✦ water-based lubricant
✦ small, blunt-ended scissors	✦ eye dropper
✦ tweezers	✦ 5ml (1 tsp) plastic syringe
✦ nail clippers	✦ sterilizing agent
✦ non-prescription soothing eye drops	✦ Elizabethan (medical) collar
	✦ surgical gloves
	✦ suitable carrier or box

IMMEDIATE ACTION

What should you do in an emergency? If the cat is in a situation where further injury could occur, such as a busy road, move the animal carefully. Depending on the position of the injuries, try to grasp the cat gently by the scruff and support its weight with the other hand. Put it in a suitable box or carrier. If the cat is unconscious, take precautions against choking by clearing any blood or vomit from the mouth and pulling the tongue forward. The head should be below the body level when the cat is lying down so that any fluids can run out.

If there is severe bleeding try to stem it by putting a pressure bandage (like a tight bandage) over the wound. This works well in areas such as the limbs. Otherwise, try applying finger pressure to the wound.

CHOKING

If a cat is fighting for air and gasping for breath, wrap it in a blanket or towel to immobilize it, and try to look in the mouth to see if there is any obstruction. While someone is calling the vet, you could try to dislocate the object by shining a small torch down the gullet and pulling the object out with a pair of tweezers. Take care you are not bitten. If a sharp object has been swallowed the problem should be dealt with by a vet. If the cat swallows a length of string or thread, do not pull it out. Leave it or tie the exposed end to an improvised collar so that it is not lost on the way to the vet.

FOREIGN BODIES

If grit, seeds or other objects become lodged in a cat's eyes or ears, you may be able to use ear or eye drops or olive oil to float them out. Do not use tweezers in these areas. A cotton bud (swab) can sometimes be used gently to remove foreign bodies in the eye.

If potentially dangerous substances such as oil, paint or chemicals are spilt on a cat's coat, wash them off immediately with a dilute solution of mild detergent or soap and water. Patches of fur that are badly soiled should be cut off carefully and the area washed with soap and water.

+ **ABOVE**
A cat that roams freely may have a more active and varied life, but it also runs a greater risk of accident and injury than the indoor pet.

+ **BELOW**
Although cats can swim – and Turkish Van cats like this one are supposed to have a particular love of water – they will drown if enough water enters the lungs.

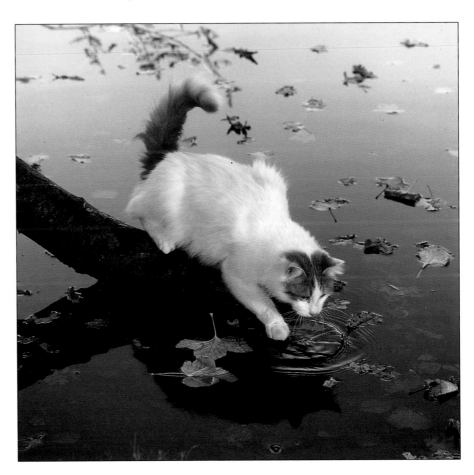

RESUSCITATION SITUATIONS

A completely collapsed cat which may appear dead can sometimes be resuscitated if you act swiftly. The condition most frequently occurs with a newly born kitten. It is very simple to assess if there is still a heartbeat by feeling for a pulse in the armpit. If no pulse is found it does not necessarily mean that brain death has occurred and you may still be able to resuscitate the animal by gently massaging the chest between finger and thumb and holding the head down.

HEART ATTACK

There has been a recent increase in the number of cats, especially pedigreed cats, who collapse and die of a condition called cardiomyopathy, of which there are various types. An apparently healthy cat may suddenly keel over and die. This condition is thought to run in families, but the mode of inheritance is unclear and is the subject of much research worldwide. Sometimes, in mild cases, massaging the chest between finger and thumb does help.

ELECTRIC SHOCK

A cat can sustain an electric shock as a result of chewing through electrical flexes and cords. Switch off the electricity immediately to prevent further shock. The vet's advice should be sought as severe burns to the gums and lips can result.

DROWNING

It takes very little liquid to cause drowning. All that is required is enough for the lungs to be filled so that oxygen is unable to enter the bloodstream. Patting the cat's back

HOW TO RESUSCITATE A CAT

There is no point in being squeamish if the cat's life is to be saved. A feline kiss of life is difficult to administer and will require coming into intimate oral contact with either the cat's nostrils or mouth. The instinct to save life is very strong so, for most owners, this aspect of resuscitation will not pose a problem.

1 Clear the airways of any vomit or blood and check that the tongue is pulled forward. Hold the cat's head gently backwards and blow into the nostrils. If the nostrils are restricted in some way, pinch the cat's mouth open with your fingers pressing both cheeks to create a restricted opening, take a deep breath and blow into the mouth. Do not overdo it, as a cat's lungs are very much smaller than a person's.

2 Between each breath, gently massage the chest to allow the air to trickle out, and maintain a rubbing motion on the cat's chest to try to stimulate heartbeat. Keep on with the mouth-to-mouth process until the cat can breath regularly by itself. It may be that this form of resuscitation does not work, in which case heart massage is the last option.

3 Heart massage may damage the cat. A delicate rubbing motion will just not stimulate the heart into beating so, with the cat on its side, preferably supported on a blanket or towel, press downwards firmly on the chest just behind the front leg, about once a second. In some cases, ribs have been broken in elderly animals, but the cat has survived. If this does not work, at least you know that you have done everything possible.

may be all that is needed to expel the water from the lungs, but more often drastic measures have to be employed such as swinging the cat by the hind legs in an attempt to get the liquid out. Then resuscitation can begin (*see box*).

ANIMAL BITES

The cat that roams freely outside is much more likely to come into contact with other animals than the house-bound feline. Fights over territorial rights around the home are likely. The bite of any animal, including other cats, dogs, rodents and snakes, can be dangerous, as many bacteria are carried in the mouth.

It may not be immediately obvious that your cat has been bitten. Usually a cat that has been hurt will find a quiet, secluded spot to lick its wounds, quite literally. This is the cat's own first aid, as its saliva contains a natural antiseptic. You may not discover a

◆ LEFT
An Elizabethan (medical) collar is attached around the neck to prevent a cat from reaching back or down to lick a wound or medical dressing. The cat's owner then has to take on all grooming responsibilities.

IMMOBILIZING A CAT THAT IS FRIGHTENED OR IN PAIN

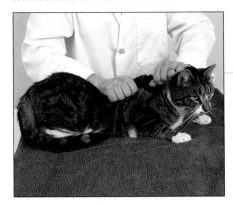

1 Place the towel on a table and the cat on the towel. Place one hand firmly on the cat's neck to control its head. Press the other firmly on the cat's back so that it lies down.

2 Keep one hand firmly on the cat's neck so that the head is under control throughout. With the other hand, bring the towel over the cat's neck, legs and body so that the legs are restrained.

3 Still keeping a firm but gentle hold on the neck, tuck the towel underneath the cat's body. Do not forget to talk to your pet in a calm voice all the time you are doing this.

hidden bite until you actually touch the site of the wound and the cat reacts. Keep the cat warm and comfortable and seek advice. Delay could mean that the cat will develop infection which will make treatment more complicated and therefore more traumatic for the cat. Wounds will need regular cleaning and bathing with a suitable antiseptic.

ABSCESSES

Any untreated puncture wound is liable to become infected and result in an abscess, which is a large, pus-filled swelling. Without treatment, the abscess may eventually burst, with a real risk of septicaemia (blood

poisoning) due to toxins from the untreated abscess entering the bloodstream. The original puncture wounds soon heal, so the correct treatment will involve a trip to the vet so that the abscess can be lanced, allowing it to drain properly.

Septicaemia is serious, as it is with people. The onset is rapid and within hours a cat can be running a very high temperature. This may be followed by fits, sickness, a rapid fall of temperature to sub-normal level, collapse and death.

The greatest cause of an abscess is a bite or claw puncture from another cat. Such wounds are invariably sustained during a fight, so the most

common abscess sites are around the head and neck, paws, and at the base of the tail.

SNAKE BITES

Many snake bites can be poisonous and may be followed by swelling around the wound, progressive lethargy and hyperventilation which may be accompanied by fits, followed by collapse and coma.

Once the wound site has been identified, try to apply a tourniquet above the punctures as quickly as possible (*see box*). The most likely site of a bite is on the leg, near the paws, in which case the tourniquet should be applied to the upper leg. If the wound is around the face or neck, then there is little that can be done.

When applying a tourniquet to a snake bite, the aim is to prevent the venom entering the bloodstream. However, remember that the application of a tourniquet cuts off the blood supply to the limb. The tourniquet should therefore be slackened every two to three minutes to ensure that the tissues are kept alive, even if this results in releasing a limited amount of the venom into the bloodstream. If this is not done, there is a possibility of such severe tissue damage that the limb would have to be amputated.

TO APPLY A TOURNIQUET

1 Place a loop of soft, narrow fabric, such as a stocking or a tie, around the limb, on the heart side of the wound site

2 Insert a pen, pencil, piece of cutlery or thin, strong stick between the skin and the fabric loop

3 Twist the fabric until it is tight enough to cut off the blood supply below it

4 Loosen the tourniquet for a few moments every two or three minutes and then re-tighten

5 If there is any swelling, apply a cold compress by wrapping a few ice cubes in a cloth, or (an athlete's tip) use a packet of frozen peas

6 Gently wash the affected spot with a recommended antiseptic, diluted to the manufacturer's instruction

7 Any bleeding should stop. If it does not, the tourniquet is not tight enough

8 Try to bandage the wound and take the cat to the vet as soon as possible. The wound may need stitching

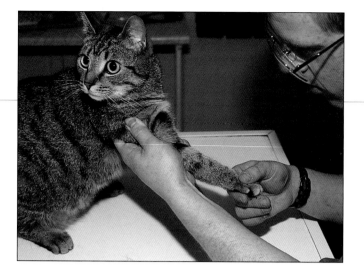

◆ BELOW
If your cat is limping, the first action to take is to examine the paw for any foreign body, such as glass or a thorn, which may be lodged there.

◆ LEFT
A vet feels a cat's leg for any breakages in the bone or internal swellings that might suggest a sprain or arthritis, to find the cause of a limp.

STINGS

It is the cat's nature to chase and pounce on insects regardless of any danger. A single wasp sting is not too alarming but remember the wasp is able to sting repeatedly. Although a cat moves fast, a wasp tangled in the cat's fur can sting a number of times before it can be brushed off. In contrast, the bee leaves the sting behind in the cat. The bee sacrifices itself when it stings, and the full quota of bee venom is left behind. Stings can occur in the mouth or throat if the insect is swallowed. This will cause swelling, and breathing and swallowing might be restricted. If external this is unpleasant and painful; internally, it can be dangerous.

The cat may show an alarming allergic reaction to a sting. If the swelling has been caused by a bee sting, the actual sting remnant may be visible. This must be removed if possible, with tweezers. Whether the sting is internal or external, the cat should have veterinary attention without delay.

As a first-aid measure, external stings by bees or wasps may be treated with a commercially available antihistamine cream or lotion. If this is not immediately available, simple home remedies can be used. Bee stings can be treated with alkaline substances such as bicarbonate of soda, whereas wasp stings respond to the application of an acid such as vinegar. The cat should not be allowed to lick at any of these substances.

POISONING

Cats are great wanderers and they may well walk through any range of toxic materials. Transferred to the mouth through washing, such substances can easily cause poisoning, and burning to contact areas. Thorough washing of paws with a mild shampoo followed by thorough rinsing will alleviate some of the pain before the vet is involved. Vomiting, lassitude, apparent blindness, convulsions and collapse are all signs of poisoning. If such symptoms occur, seek veterinary aid immediately.

It is inadvisable to try to find a way of easing the animal's suffering yourself beyond keeping the cat warm and quiet. Take a sample of the substance if you know what it is, or note the name, so that an antidote may be found quickly if available. Your vet will have access to the national poison hotline. In some countries, where stray animals are a

◆ ABOVE
Give a cat a toy to play with in the garden, and with a bit of luck, this may distract it from pursuing the local wildlife.

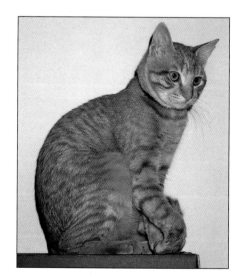

◆ ABOVE
A vital nerve was severed in this cat's foreleg. The cause was barely visible – a tiny puncture in the skin, perhaps from a barbed wire fence or an animal bite. There was no improvement after a month, and the leg was amputated, but the cat continued to lead an active outdoor life.

BANDAGING A LEG

1 One person should hold the cat, and the other apply the dressing. Place lint over the injured area and hold it in place with your hand.

2 Use the bandage to bind the lint into position by taking it down over the paw and back up again; then wind it around the leg.

3 Continue winding the bandage firmly (but not so tight that the blood supply is cut off) and evenly around the entire length of the leg.

4 Split the end of the bandage leaving two ends long enough to take back around the leg in opposite directions. Tie the two ends together.

5 Tape adhesive bandage over the end of the paw and back up again as before. Wind around the entire length of the leg.

6 Keep the cat indoors for as long as the dressing is on. Change the dressing regularly as advised by the vet, or when it becomes grubby or loose.

nuisance, cats and dogs are sometimes deliberately poisoned by those who consider them pests.

If your cat returns home covered in motor oil, it is important to remove the oil from the coat immediately, as it could poison the cat's digestive system and result in kidney damage. Use a mild household detergent in lots of warm water, and seek veterinary advice if in difficulty.

SCRAPES AND BRUISES

Bruises are much less easy to detect than cuts, though you will suspect their presence if the cat becomes unusually unhappy about your touching the spot where the bruise is rooted. Similar signs are apparent if an abscess is developing on the site. As with human bruises, some come to the surface of the skin reasonably rapidly, whereas deep-seated bruising can take days to work its way out. Seek professional advice if

in doubt. Bruises and contusions respond very well to the application of *Hamamelis virginiana* (witch-hazel). Although such a remedy can be taken orally in very limited doses, it is better to prevent the cat from licking off any application by putting a medical collar around the neck.

STRAINS AND LIMPS

The cat may limp and resort to excessive washing of the injured spot. If you suspect something is amiss, first examine the paw carefully to see if there is a splinter or thorn in it, and remove it with tweezers if possible. Disinfect the area and keep your eye on the cat. Confine the cat indoors, and if there is no improvement, ask the vet to have a look at it.

If the problem is a strain, a cat will not rest of its own accord, and continued physical activity could not only aggravate the strain but also prevent it from healing.

BURNS

Cats attracted by cooking smells may leap on to unguarded cooking areas and even into ovens, and may be scalded by spilled hot liquid. A cat may also receive appalling burns, externally and internally, if it comes into contact with any of the lethal chemicals to be found in the house and garden.

Once the skin is burned, the body institutes its own first-aid regime. Body fluids are rushed to the affected area, and a blister forms protecting the underlying tissue. Do not burst the blister as the fluid in it helps to prevent infection. You can bathe the burn with ice-cold water until all heat has been taken out of the damaged area. Call the vet.

You can also apply a sterile, dry dressing loosely over the burn to keep out infection. Do not apply greasy substances – this would be like putting butter into a hot frying pan.

VIRAL INFECTIONS

Viruses need a host body to provide the energy they need to reproduce. Not all viruses cause disease. In the cat, pathogenic (disease-producing) viruses are responsible for such serious conditions as feline enteritis, cat flu and rabies. Some viruses, such as the one responsible for enteritis, are stable and resilient, surviving for long periods, while others, such as the flu virus, are readily destroyed by common disinfectants. Some viruses produce acute disease very quickly, while others have a long incubation period, like the feline immunodeficiency virus (FIV).

Even though you are able to protect your cat from many serious viral infections by means of vaccination, it is not yet universally common veterinary practice to inoculate against rabies or feline infectious peritonitis. Both vaccines are available worldwide but not necessarily universally licensed. In the United Kingdom, for example, the rabies virus is only used on animals intended for export. If, as is predicted, quarantine regulations are lifted in Britain, vaccination is likely to become mandatory. The viral diseases that are effectively protected against by vaccination include feline enteritis and the flu viruses.

Infections are not necessarily the same as disease. Disease is any impairment of the normal functioning of the animal, and is usually, but not always, caused by infection. For example, cats will become infected with feline coronavirus, but may not show any signs of disease or illness at all. Infections are not always contagious, that is, they need not spread to other animals by contact.

CHLAMYDIA

Chlamydial organisms fall midway between viruses and bacteria (which, unlike viruses, are self-contained cells and do not need a host body) and are responsible for a disease of the upper respiratory tract in the cat, with symptoms very similar to those of cat flu. Minor outbreaks cause one or both eyes to become inflamed and to show an unpleasant discharge. More severe attacks also cause nasal discharge and a subsequent loss of smell and appetite. Chlamydia organisms are susceptible to similar antibiotics to which bacteria are sensitive. A vaccine has been available since 1991, and though the majority of cases are observed in households with pedigreed breeding stock, it is certainly known in the wider cat population.

INFLUENZA (VIRAL RHINITIS)

This is a distressing illness affecting the upper respiratory tract, which is caused by two main viruses, feline calicivirus and feline herpesvirus. Both viruses cause coughing and sneezing. Discharge from the nose and the eyes cause the cat great distress, and a rasping soreness in the throat discourages eating or drinking. Feline calicivirus often causes serious ulceration of nose, mouth and tongue. Feline herpesvirus may cause the nose, windpipe and lungs to become

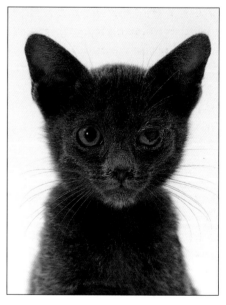

✦ ABOVE
The acute conjunctivitis and corneal opacity in one of this Blue Tonkinese kitten's eyes are symptoms of chlamydia, a respiratory disease.

◆ RIGHT
A Lilac Cream Burmese-cross kitten has severe conjunctivitis – a symptom of feline flu.

seriously inflamed, resulting in a lot of coughing and sneezing. The cat that is kept warm and comfortable and is encouraged to eat and drink stands the greatest chance of survival. Antibiotics reduce the risk of secondary infections but do not attack the primary viruses. Effective vaccination against cat flu is the best preventative course.

FELINE INFECTIOUS ENTERITIS

This disease, a cat version of the distemper that infects dogs, is also known as feline panleukopaenia and feline parvovirus. The first symptom of this sometimes astonishingly rapid killer virus is usually a very high fever. The virus attacks rapidly dividing cells, particularly in the bowel. Symptoms may include unusually depressed behaviour, loss of appetite, vomiting, and a desire to drink but an inability to do so. Diarrhoea is not always present. Rapid dehydration sets in followed by coma and death. The rapidity of the disease, after its short incubation period, can mean that death occurs two or three days after vomiting starts or even within 24 hours. The disease is highly infectious. Treatment is supportive: keep the cat warm and free from draughts, and administer re-hydration therapy as advised by the vet.

FELINE LEUKAEMIA VIRUS (FeLV)

This virus first came to the notice of breeders of pedigreed cats in the early 1970s. Originally there were fears that it could be a health hazard to humans, particularly children. This is most certainly not the case – the virus cannot be transmitted except to another cat. To begin with, it was thought that particular pedigreed

breeds were more prone to the disease than other cats, but this has not been proven. All cats may be similarly and as rapidly affected when they come into contact with the virus. It was found that a far larger percentage of the normal domestic cat population was affected than expected, and many of these cats lived into old age. This made a nonsense of early veterinary advice that cats with feline leukaemia virus should be euthanased immediately.

Some cats do succumb rapidly to other serious and untreatable infections as the virus wreaks havoc with the cat's immune system, while others are less affected. If one cat is affected within a multi-cat household, it should be removed, as the virus is easily transmitted through saliva or blood. The infected animal could be moved to a single-cat household where it may live out its life without infecting others. Testing for the virus

is through a blood sample. It is possible for a cat to test positive and then, two weeks later, to show a negative result, only having had a passing contact with the virus. For some years, a vaccine countering this disease has been available in the United States, and since 1992, FeLV licences have been available in the United Kingdom.

Most breeders have all their animals, whether elderly, neutered (altered) or young breeding cats, regularly tested to show that they are FeLV-negative. Females are only mated to males which also regularly test negative, so that the kittens are automatically negative too. They can then be protected by vaccination. Many breeders leave this to the new owners. If there are other cats in your home, it should be done immediately. If the kitten is the only pet, inoculation may be left until it is a little older.

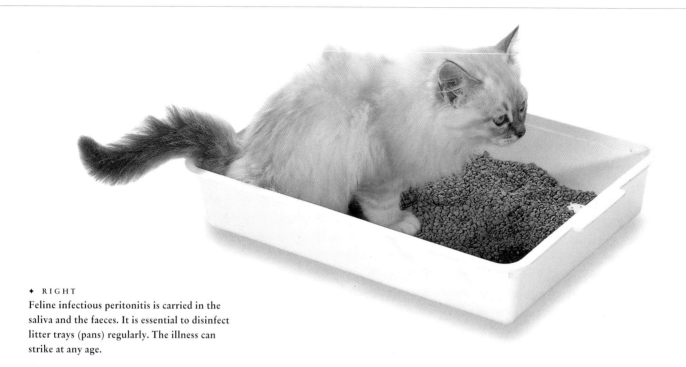

◆ RIGHT
Feline infectious peritonitis is carried in the saliva and the faeces. It is essential to disinfect litter trays (pans) regularly. The illness can strike at any age.

FELINE IMMUNODEFICIENCY VIRUS (FIV)

This is a similar virus to the human immunodeficiency virus (HIV) which may lead eventually to acquired immunodeficiency syndrome (AIDS). The feline version cannot be passed on to a human being, and HIV cannot be passed on to a cat.

FIV progressively breaks down the cat's immune system. This leads to the cat becoming increasingly vulnerable to infections. Despite periods of apparently normal health, the cat slowly succumbs to minor illnesses which become untreatable. No vaccination exists at present.

FELINE INFECTIOUS PERITONITIS (FIP)

The virus that causes this disease is found in many cats and normally only occasionally causes a transient diarrhoea. However, in about 10 per cent of infected cats, the virus leaves the intestines, invades the blood

vessels and causes a severe inflammation – which is feline infectious peritonitis. The membrane which lines the abdominal cavity is called the peritoneum, and once the

◆ ABOVE
A cat is spending a night in the vet's pens before surgery in the morning.

blood vessels of this have become infected and inflamed, treatment is extremely difficult, and often unsuccessful. As yet no definitive pattern to the progression of illness has emerged. The disease can be triggered in almost all age groups, even young kittens are susceptible.

Wet FIP is the most common form of the disease. Onset is usually rapid. Just 24 hours after appearing lively, playful, of good appetite and with normal litter-tray (pan) motions, a wet FIP sufferer will be lethargic, will not want to eat very much and will have sickness and diarrhoea. The coat is often staring and dull, but the most dramatic sign is the grossly distended fluid-filled abdomen. There is no cure. Euthanasia is the only option.

Dry FIP is a less common form of the disease and is often difficult to diagnose. The signs are similar to those of other illnesses. Terminally, the cat may have jaundice and show symptoms akin to cat flu, physical disorientation, blindness due to haemorrhages in the eyes and, finally, fits.

The presence of the virus is detected by antibody tests. Cats which show none are designated nil titre count. Over 80 per cent of show cats are seropositive, showing they have had some contact with the disease. Some cat breeders advertise their animals as nil (free) status, but most vets regard a low count as being relatively normal. Many cats, even with a very high titre count may seem normal. It is thought that a stressful situation, such as the introduction of a new cat into the household or a long journey, may tip a cat with a pre-existing viral condition into the full-blown illness.

FIP does not seem to be as infectious as was at first thought. The virus is carried in the cat's saliva and the faeces. Litter trays (pans) should be disinfected regularly and frequently using an agent recommended by your vet. Keeping cats in small, easily managed colonies, observing strict hygiene and, above all, maintaining a stress-free environment should help reduce the possibility of the disease flaring up. The virus is not able to survive very long outside the host and is very susceptible to disinfection agents. There is no vaccination available at present in the United Kingdom although it is available in some European countries.

RABIES

All mammals, including humans, are susceptible to rabies, and the bite of an infected animal is dangerous. Once infected, a cat may show signs of a radical alteration of appetite and voice, with unexpected aggressive behaviour. An inability to drink gives rabies its other name, hydrophobia – fear of water. Other signs follow – foaming at the mouth, swelling of the skull, jaw paralysis and disorientation.

Treatment is possible but must be started promptly after being bitten by a suspected animal. There is very little hope of any infected mammal surviving once the long incubation period of the disease has passed and symptoms have begun to show. Several countries are rabies-free, including the United Kingdom due to rigorous import regulations. Vaccination is available and standard in countries where rabies exists but, at present, in Britain it is only obtainable for animals that are to be exported.

FELINE SPONGIFORM ENCEPHALOPATHY

This disease is caused by a sub-viral protein that is capable of reproducing itself. It is similar to the bovine form (BSE) that has occurred in the United Kingdom, but not elsewhere. The disease seems to be invariably fatal in cats, and is not diagnosable prior to death. It seems to have been transmitted to cats as a result of eating meat from cattle infected with BSE or sheep with scrapie. The cat develops abnormal behaviour, including failure to groom, and often drools with muscle tremors and an abnormal head posture. However, positive diagnosis is only possible on post-mortem examination.

♦ LEFT
One of the early signs of the feline form of BSE is a disinterest in grooming.

PARASITES

Being aware of the problems and facts about parasites is the first step in prevention. Routine care of any cat or kitten must include checking that the fur and skin are kept free from all parasites.

A parasite is an animal or plant that takes food and protection from a host animal or plant. It survives to the detriment of its host, causing loss of condition, and sometimes death. In some cases, such as ringworm, the parasitic condition of a host cat can be passed on to the humans it lives with.

Preparations to eradicate external parasites such as fleas, ticks, lice, mites and ringworm, as well as internal parasites including worms, are easily available. Ask veterinary advice, follow

✦ ABOVE
A cat is having its regular check for fleas, lice, and ticks. The check-up can be part of a weekly grooming routine.

instructions carefully, and stick to a strict cleaning regime, and parasites should not be a problem.

FLEAS

The cat with fleas may scratch obsessively, particularly around the neck, and may groom the base of the spine vigorously and spontaneously. It may also worry at the entire length of the spine. Using the tips of the fingers and nails, groom the cat behind the ears, the neck, spine and base of the tail. If this reveals dark, chocolate-brown grit, put these on a damp tissue. If red leaches from them, they are flea droppings, which are largely made up of dried blood.

In severe infestations or where the cat is actually allergic to substances produced by the flea in its bite, patches of scabby skin may be found with the scabs breaking off to reveal sore-looking, slightly weeping patches. This clears up rapidly with the eradication of the fleas.

Fleas move very fast through the fur of the cat and are difficult to catch even if seen. A cat can be attacked by

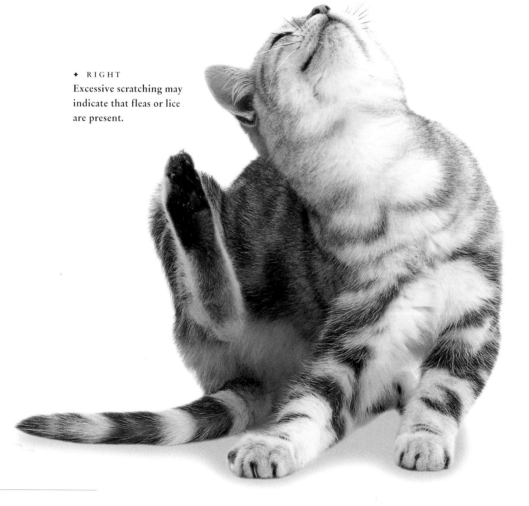

✦ RIGHT
Excessive scratching may indicate that fleas or lice are present.

the cat flea, the dog flea and the human flea. They all lay their eggs in the cat's fur; many will drop out and hatch into larvae in cracks in the floorboards, in the weave of fabrics and in carpets. The larvae develop into fleas that immediately feed from any host that may wander by. A flea can live, with periods of feeding and resting, for up to two years, but two to six months is the norm.

Many anti-parasitic preparations, including powders, shampoos and sprays are available from pet stores, supermarkets and veterinary practices. With heavy infestations, both the cat and the environment have to be treated. Long-acting sprays are probably the most effective for the environment. For the cat, one of the easiest and most effective methods is an insecticide that is applied to a small area on the cat's neck. This spot application gives protection to the whole body for a month.

Modern parasiticides are very safe and some are available that can be applied to very young kittens. Your vet will advise on the most appropriate products for young cats.

TICKS

Ticks, like fleas, are blood suckers. However, unlike fleas, they live permanently on the cat. This parasite is normally rural in distribution, but the hedgehog tick is common in urban areas. The tick burrows its head into the host animal's skin, and gorges itself on blood. It can sometimes reach the size of a haricot bean, then drop off to complete its life cycle with no further damage to the cat. However, it could move on to other animals in the home. Removal of a tick requires

precision, to avoid the head parts remaining buried in the skin. The cat itself may be irritated by the tick's burrowing and knock it off, leaving its head behind. This usually sets up chronic infection followed by an abscess or sore which is difficult to heal. A vet can use substances to relax the tick's hold before removing it. A home equivalent is surgical alcohol (or any form of alcoholic spirit). The whole tick is then carefully removed with tweezers or a custom-made tick remover (available from pet stores).

Tick bites can be responsible for a bacterial disease called Lyme disease. This occurs in Britain, but is more widespread in the United States. Symptoms include a reluctance to jump followed by acute and recurring lameness, a raised temperature, lethargy and swollen lymph nodes, particularly around the head and

limbs. Blood tests confirm the cause, and treatment is a four to six week course of antibiotics. Lyme disease should not occur if ticks are prevented. Most flea preparations also prevent tick infestation.

LICE

Fortunately, lice infestation is uncommon on cats, but poor condition and extremes of age make individuals susceptible. There are three types of louse which are known to occur on cats, one blood-sucking, and two which bite. Telltale signs are some scratching, usually not very excessive, combined with dry skin which shows an unusual increase of scurf or dandruff. The lice may be seen quite easily with the naked eye. The eggs, or nits, are laid directly on the lower third of the hair and seem to be glued in place. Anti-flea preparations are effective.

◆ ABOVE, LEFT AND RIGHT
As a preventative measure against fleas and lice, apply an anti-parasite insecticide once a month. Part the fur on the back of the neck and squeeze on the required amount of medication.

✦ BELOW
Incessant scratching of the head and ears is a sign of ear mites, and could aggravate the problem if not treated quickly.

MITES

Four groups of mites affect the cat's skin and ears. The harvest mite appears in the autumn (fall). The cat is affected by the larvae which tend to settle in areas where the fur is thin, such as between the toes, on the underbelly, in the groin and around the lips and nose.

The orange larvae are just about visible to the naked eye. They set up irritation which the cat vigorously attacks with teeth and claws, thus creating more irritation. The sores which develop are round, damp and surrounded by scabby skin. Mite infestation is highly contagious and treated with insecticidal preparations.

The ear mite is commonly transmitted from cat to cat. Irritation is sometimes severe; the cat shakes its head, holds the ears almost flat, and scratches furiously. This often leads to secondary infections arising from self-inflicted trauma. Evidence of ear mites is a dark brown tarry substance

in the ears. Because of the ear's delicacy, it is wise to ask your vet to carry out initial treatment. The owner can then cleanse the ear gently.

Cheyletiella mites cause a condition known as "walking dandruff", and are less common. They often seem to cause little irritation to the cat though

there may be more scratching and grooming than usual. Excessive dandruff is the usual sign. The mite normally lives on the wild rabbit and can also affect people (rashes appear on chest, stomach and arms). Treatment is with parasiticides – for both cat and human!

One fortunately rare form of mange is caused by a burrowing mite. It is usually found around the head starting at the base of the ear. There is severe irritation, hair loss and general lack of condition. Blood poisoning can occur in severe cases. Antibiotic treatment is necessary for any secondary infections, while the actual skin damage is treated with the use of parasiticidal preparations.

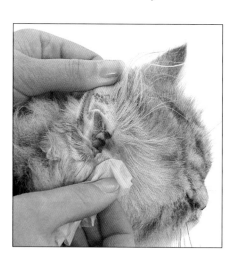

✦ ABOVE
Regular checking and cleaning at grooming time will keep mite infestations at bay.

✦ RIGHT
A vet checks for ear mites as part of the routine examination.

RINGWORM

Ringworm is caused by a fungus, and can affect humans, especially children. The name comes from the shape of the lesions seen on the skin in humans, which are circular, red, scaly and very itchy. In the cat, particularly the

Persian, often all that is seen are tiny pimples and scurf on the skin. (Nevertheless, these cats can still be highly contagious.) At worst, moist, pink sores spread outwards. The fungal parasite lives on the hair and not on the skin, and causes the hair to break off. Ringworm can affect animals that are not in top condition, or that are young, and can be a major problem in longhaired show cats.

Diagnosis is initially by the use of special filtered light (Wood's Light), when about 65 per cent of cases will fluoresce. Laboratory tests are more reliable but take longer. The eradication process is long and tedious. The animals are treated with fungicides, both in the form of baths and external applications, and also tablets. The entire environment, human and animal, has to be carefully cleansed to eradicate all spores. There is no simple answer to the problem. Professional advice on procedure must be taken and, if necessary, the local environmental health department consulted. In the United States and in the United Kingdom, research is aimed at improving diagnostic tests as well as treatments. Considerable headway has been made in the production of a vaccine, but at present only cuts down treatment time.

MAGGOTS

Flies may be attracted to animals by the presence of discharge from wounds, or diarrhoea, and lay their eggs in the fur. Fly strike, as this situation is known, is particularly common in cats in poor condition, such as those in feral colonies. The maggots burrow into the skin and form tunnels which can run for considerable distances. Toxins produced to aid burrowing are absorbed by the cat and cause toxaemia (blood poisoning). If you find maggot infestation on your cat, clean it as thoroughly as possible using soap and water and contact the vet without delay.

BRONCHITIS

Infectious bronchitis is sometimes caused by a parasitic bacterium that lodges in the respiratory tract of animals. The parasite itself does not normally cause disease, but certain strains of the parasite do cause bronchitis. In a dog, this may appear as kennel cough. A cat on the other hand may cough and sneeze, with or without running nose and eyes. Normally, the disease is self-limiting. However, in very young or elderly cats, or those with other debilitating diseases, it can be persistent and troublesome to clear. The organism is sensitive to several antibiotics.

◆ BELOW LEFT
Thinning and bald patches on the hind leg of a Blue Burmese could be signs of ringworm.

◆ BELOW RIGHT
The mark on the head of this Lilac Tonkinese kitten is confirmed as ringworm. The fungal parasites live on the hair, and not on the skin, causing the hair to break.

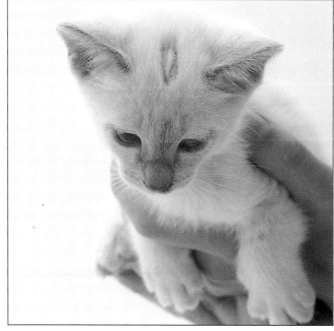

WORMS

The cat is affected by two groups of internal, parasitic worm – roundworms and tapeworms. Effective worm treatments are available, without prescription, from pet stores and supermarkets. However, experience has shown that these may be difficult to administer with total accuracy. Routine worming treatments – and advice – are best obtained from your vet. Worming preparations which give multiple protection to the cat are now available either as tablets or injections. Regular, correctly spaced treatments will keep your cat worm-free. These are often supplied at the same time as the annual booster vaccination, but may need to be given every six months.

ROUNDWORMS

Roundworms include ascarids, hookworms and lungworms. Infestations are difficult to spot unless the attack is severe, in which case, especially with ascarids, a ball of living worms may be voided. If you suspect infestation, you will probably need to take a faecal sample to the vet for accurate identification. Ascarids and hookworms live in the small intestine. They have very similar life cycles but whereas the ascarids are free-floating and feed on food in the process of digestion, the hookworms attach themselves to the lining of the intestine and suck blood. Symptoms are, therefore, slightly different. In a severe ascarid infestation, the cat will have diarrhoea, the coat will be lank, and the cat will generally look uncomfortable. Often the belly is distended ("pot belly").

The main symptom of hookworm infestation is anaemia, which in a cat is most obvious on its nose leather and gums. The gums appear excessively pale, almost white. There is a general

♦ LEFT
A vet checks gum and tongue colour for any undue paleness that could indicate anaemia and possible hookworm infestation.

lack of energy and the cat may become very thin.

The intermediate host of the lungworm is the slug or snail, which could be eaten by a cat. However, it is more likely that they will be eaten first by birds or rodents and the infective larvae reach the cat through eating them. Nevertheless, infestation is quite rare. After a complicated journey through the cat's intestine and lymph nodes, the larvae become adult worms, which eventually enter the lungs via the bloodstream. As a result, respiratory symptoms occur, similar to bronchitis or pneumonia.

TAPEWORMS

Tapeworm diagnosis is relatively easy. Segments of tapeworm containing eggs are shed and attach themselves to the fur around the anus. They look like grains of rice. Tapeworms require intermediate hosts and the flea fulfils this role in relation to the most common tapeworm to affect the cat. Flea control is therefore important. Flea larvae eat the secreted tapeworm segments that contain the eggs. The infective stage of the tapeworm is reached as the adult flea preys on the cat for a blood meal. If the cat catches and swallows the flea, as it may do

while grooming, the process is completed. The infective stage of the second most common tapeworm to affect cats develops in the livers of small rodents. The infected livers and other intestinal parts will almost certainly be consumed by a cat, if it catches one of these animals.

The way to prevent infestation by tapeworms is to eradicate fleas, and discourage your cat from hunting. Both may be impossible targets, but although tapeworms continue to be a problem, their presence does not seem to affect cats much beyond diarrhoea in the case of very heavy infestation.

♦ RIGHT
The abdomen of a cat being palpated; a distended belly may indicate roundworm infestation.

I N J U R I E S A N D A I L M E N T S

◆ BELOW
Keep an eye open for roving cats using your
garden as a toileting area. Your animals may be
free of diseases such as toxoplasmosis, but
visitors may not be.

TOXOPLASMOSIS

Toxoplasmosis is caused by microscopic organisms called coccidia. The organisms can infect humans, although symptoms of illness are rarely felt. If a pregnant woman is infected, however, the foetus may be affected, resulting in spontaneous abortion or brain damage to the baby. The disease may not even affect the cat in any recognizable form, although it may cause a chest infection in young cats. In older cats there may be gross loss of condition, digestive disorders and anaemia. Eye problems are not uncommon.

The immature egg of the parasite is passed in the cat's faeces, so that potential contact with any faecal matter when changing and cleaning litter trays (pans) must be countered by a rigid routine of hygiene. Oocysts passed by the cat with toxoplasmosis take at least 24 hours to become infective, so litter trays (pans) must be changed as soon as possible after use and rubber gloves worn.

Small children should be kept away from litter trays (pans) at all times. You should also frequently clear away the faeces of any neighbourhood cats that visit your garden and use it as a toileting area.

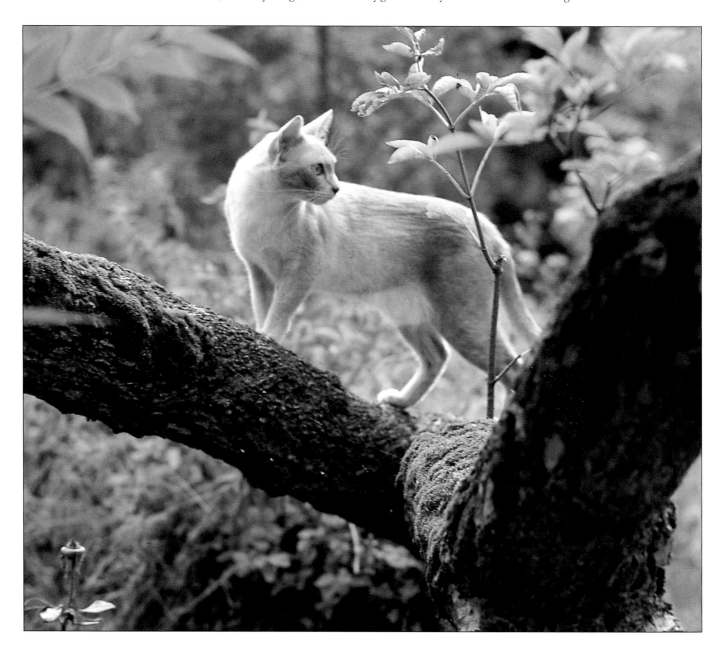

AREAS AFFECTED

EYES

Conjunctivitis is relatively common in the cat and can vary from a relatively mild infection often called "gum eye" by cat breeders to more serious conditions such as that caused by the chlamydia organism.

Gum eye is mostly seen in kittens just after their eyes have opened at about seven to ten days, up until the age of about three weeks. The eyes appear to be firmly glued together with a discharge and this may be due to a mild viral infection. Usually, the mother cat will wash the eyes open, but sometimes you will have to help her. To do this, bathe the kitten's eye(s) with a sterile pad soaked in cold water. Always work from the corner of the eye nearest the nose outwards. Should the gum eye persist over a couple of days, seek professional advice.

EARS

A blood blister called a haematoma can occur on the ear flap (pinna) due to excessive shaking and rubbing caused by irritation. Without skilled treatment, a deformed pinna will result in cauliflower ear.

NOSE

Nasal discharges are usually due to viral infections like cat flu and should be treated by the vet. Certain breeds of cat (Persians, in particular) have restricted nostrils, and the flattening, or foreshortening, of the face causes kinking of the tear duct. The cat will probably always have eye and nasal discharges that have to be constantly attended to by the owner. Rarely, a cat may show an asthmatic condition, having become allergic to

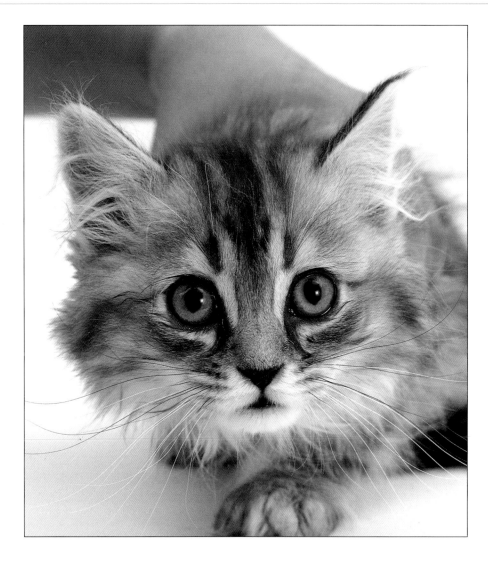

one or more of the thousands of substances it encounters each day. Again, your vet should be able to diagnose and may even pinpoint the allergen. Long-term treatment may be necessary.

CHEST AND LUNGS

Inflammation of the fine membrane that covers the lungs and inside of the chest cavity is called pleurisy. Cats may have fluid in their chests for various reasons, ranging from heart failure to injuries. Usually, the fluid is sterile, but it may become infected with certain bacteria, either blood-

borne or from a bite or wound. Breathing becomes increasingly difficult, and any sudden exercise results in panting and a wide-eyed, very distressed appearance. The condition needs urgent veterinary attention, and despite chest drains and antibiotic treatment, many cats do not respond, and die of the condition known as pyothorax.

SKIN

Cats can sometimes develop a type of acne, in which blackheads appear on the chin. These are caused by excessive production and secretion of

◆ RIGHT
A young owner tries
to entice her cat to
come out of the
carrier on its annual
trip to the vet.

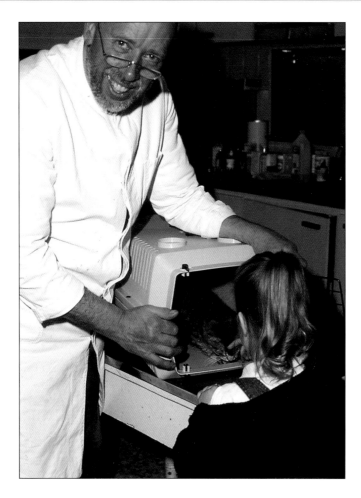

◆ RIGHT
A young owner tries
to entice her cat to
come out of the
carrier on its annual
trip to the vet.

◆ BELOW LEFT
Checking mouth,
gums and teeth is a
vital part of the
annual check-up.

◆ BELOW RIGHT
The vet uses an
ophthalmoscope
to check the
cat's eyes.

sebum, which lubricates the hair. The pores through which the sebum is released may become blocked. When it occurs on the top of the tail it is known as "stud tail". Both conditions should be treated with antibiotics and anti-inflammatory drugs. If your cat has a predisposition for these conditions, keep both areas scrupulously clean to prevent recurrence, and if in any doubt, consult the vet.

Even the best groomed cat can be affected by dandruff. When it strikes, even a shorthaired cat needs to be bathed and a conditioning agent used. If the scurf persists despite your best efforts, there may be something actually wrong with the skin itself.

DIGESTIVE SYSTEM

Constipation and diarrhoea often occur during the life of any otherwise healthy cat. There are

◆ ABOVE
The vet palpates (feels) the cat's abdomen to make sure that it is neither swollen nor tender, and also the glands around the neck and top of the legs to make sure they are not enlarged.

◆ RIGHT
The vet administers ear drops to a cat with a sore ear. The ears are very delicate, so it is always preferable for the vet to check them initially if you think there is a problem.

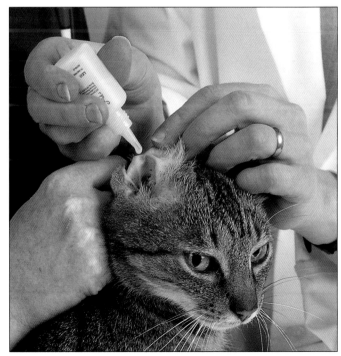

many reasons why a cat becomes constipated. Fur balls (hairballs) are a usual cause, but sometimes a diet with insufficient bulk or roughage (see the chapter *Nutrition and Feeding*) may be the problem. Introduce some bran or other cereal into the diet, or add a little liquid paraffin to the food. If the condition persists, take the cat to the vet. It may indicate a more serious condition, such as megacolon. If too much liquid paraffin is used, the cat will have diarrhoea.

There are feline preparations on the market, but home-made remedies are often just as effective. These involve a mild diet of bland food which does not upset the system. Try feeding the cat cooked white meat and white fish bulked out with simple boiled rice or pasta. Some cats adore natural yogurt. Another remedy is to sprinkle dehydrated potato granules on the food – it may seem unorthodox, but it works.

With both constipation and diarrhoea, the anal glands, which are situated on either side of the anal opening, may become blocked, infected and swell up. Clearing them out can be done at home, but it is not pleasant and does require some skill, so it is probably better left to a professional.

In addition to being uncomfortable, excessive diarrhoea or straining can cause a condition called anal prolapse. This can easily be recognized – a small section of the bowel protrudes through the anal opening. Do not do anything about this yourself; a vet must immediately put this back into its proper place, possibly with a stitch or two to secure it.

INDEX

Acknowledgements

The publishers would like
to thank Paddy Cutts for
her invaluable help.

The photographer and
publishers would like to
thank the following for
their assistance with the
photography: Paddy
Cutts, Alison Hay, S. and
R. Badger, S. Bagley, G.
Black, V. Dyer, C. Fry,
Wade and Kirby Heames,
H. Hewitt, B. Hollandt,
J. and D. Johnson, R.
Lowen, B. and L. Riddy,
Pampered Pets, Colin
Clark veterinary practice,
Burntwood boarding
cattery, Weycolour Ltd.